BEING THERE

THE BENEFITS OF A STAY-AT-HOME PARENT

By Isabelle Fox, Ph.D.

With Norman M. Lobsenz

BARRON'S

Dedication

To my husband—Robert who is always "there" for all of us.

About the Author

Isabelle Fox, Ph.D. received degrees from Radcliffe College and UCLA. For the last 30 years she has been a practicing psychotherapist in Southern California. She specializes in parent-child relationships and developmental issues. For 10 years she was a senior mental health consultant for Operation Head Start.

All inquiries should be addressed to:
Barron's Educational Series, Inc.
250 Wireless Boulevard
Hauppauge, New York 11788

Library of Congress Catalog Card No. 95-41297
International Standard Book No. 0-8120-9490-5

Library of Congress Cataloging-in-Publication Data
Fox, Isabelle.
    The importance of being there : the benefits of a stay-at-home parent / by Isabelle Fox with Norman M. Lobsenz.
        p.   cm.
    Includes bibliographical references.
    ISBN 0-8120-9490-5
    1. Parent and child. 2. Parenting. 3. Work and family.
4. Child care. 5. Children of working parents. 6. Attachment behavior in children. I. Title.
HQ755.85.F69   1996
306.874—dc20   95-41297
                                            CIP

PRINTED IN THE UNITED STATES OF AMERICA
6789   8800   987654321

Acknowledgments

The author gratefully acknowledges the following copyright holders for permission to reprint material used in this publication:

From *Attachment and Loss, Volume I: Attachment* by John Bowlby. Copyright © 1969 by Tavistock Institute of Human Relations and HarperCollins Publishers, Inc. p. 37.

From brief excerpts from *Attachment and Loss, Volume II: Separation: Anxiety & Anger* by John Bowlby. Copyright © 1973 by Tavistock Institute of Human Relations. Reprinted by permission of Basic Books, a division of HarperCollins Publishers, Inc. pp. 40, 79.

From brief excerpts from *A Secure Base* by John Bowlby. Copyright © 1988 by Richard P. J. Bowlby, Robert J. M. Bowlby and Anthony Gatlin. Reprinted by permission of Basic Books, a division of HarperCollins Publishers, Inc. and Tavistock Publications, Ltd. pp. 13, 37, 40, 41, 42, 45, 54, 59, 79.

From brief excerpts from *Diary of a Baby* by Daniel N. Stern. Copyright © 1990 by Daniel N. Stern, M.D. Reprinted by permission of Basic Books, a division of HarperCollins Publishers, Inc. pp. 8, 45.

From *A Better World for Our Children* © 1994 by Dr. Benjamin Spock. Reprinted by permission of National Press Books Inc.

Excerpt from *American Baby* magazine, October 1985, "Should You Stay Home With Your Baby?" by Burton L. White, Ph.D. Reprinted with permission of the author.

Excerpt from *Attachment in the Preschool Years* by Greenberg, Cicchetti & Cummings. Copyright © 1990 The University of Chicago Press. Reprinted with permission of The University of Chicago Press. pp. 79, 80.

Excerpts from the following articles "Infant Day Care: A Cause For Concern" and "Risks Remain" by Jay Belsky, Ph.D. as published in *Zero to Three*. Reprinted with permission of Jay Belsky, Ph.D.

From *Children First* by Penelope Leach. Copyright © 1994 by Penelope Leach. Reprinted by permission of Alfred A. Knopf Inc. pp. 8, 9, 21, 30, 31, 38, 63, 129, 130.

Excerpts from *Early Deprivation of Empathic Care* by John L. Weil. Copyright © 1992 by John L. Weil, M.D. Reprinted with permission of International Universities Press, Inc.

From *High Risk: Children Without A Conscience* by Dr. Ken Magid and Carole McKelvey. Copyright © 1987 by Dr. Ken Magid and Carole A. McKelvey. Used by permission of Bantam Books, a division of Bantam Doubleday Dell Publishing Group, Inc. pp. 37, 72, 74, 75, 78, 84, 128.

Excerpts from *Child Development—Its Nature and Course, 2nd Edition* by Sroufe, Cooper and DeHart. Copyright © 1992, 1988 by McGraw-Hill Inc. Reprinted with permission of McGraw-Hill, Inc. pp. 12, 65.

Excerpt from the article "High Risk Children in Young Adulthood: A Longitudinal Study from Birth to 32 Years" by Emmy E. Werner, Ph.D. Reprinted, with permission, from the *American Journal of Orthopsychiatry* and the author, Emmy E. Werner. Copyright 1989 by the American Orthopsychiatric Association, Inc.

From Dr. Virginia Hunter, 1991 *John Bowlby: An Interview*, Psychoanalytic Review 78(2) Summer 1991 Guilford Press. © 1991 N.P.A.P. Reprinted with permission of Dr. Virginia Hunter and The Guilford Press.

From Baron, *Growing up with Language: How Children Learn to Talk*, © 1992 Naomi S. Baron. Reprinted by permission of Addison-Wesley Publishing Company, Inc.

From a quotation by Dr. J. Ronald Lally as published in *Zero to Three* article by Chang and Pulido, Oct/Nov. 1994. Reprinted with permission of Dr. J. Ronald Lally Director—Center for Children and Family Studies—Far West Laboratory.

From *The Making and Breaking of Affectionate Bonds* by John Bowlby. © 1979 R. P. L. Bowlby and others. Reprinted with permission of Tavistock Publications Ltd.

From *Working and Caring* (pp. 56; 116), © 1987, 1985 by T. Berry Brazelton, M.D. Reprinted by permission of Addison-Wesley Publishing Company, Inc.

Quotations from The Rockford Institute's *The Family in America* publication, February 1991 "Children at Risk: The Case Against Day Care." Reprinted with permission of The Rockford Institute's *The Family in America* publication.

From Cost, Quality and Child Outcomes Study Team (1995). *Cost, Quality, and Child Outcomes in Child Care Centers, Public Report.* Denver: Economics

Department, University of Colorado at Denver. With permission of University of Colorado at Denver.

From *Monographs of the Society for Research in Child Development* 1985 Vol. 50 (1–2, 147–166), an excerpt from an article "The Relationship Between Quality of Attachment And Behavior Problems In Preschool In A High Risk Sample." © The Society for Research in Child Development, Inc. Reprinted with permission.

Excerpt from *Every Child's Birthright: In Defense of Mothering* by Selma Fraiberg. Copyright © 1977 by Selma Fraiberg. Reprinted with permission of HarperCollins Publishers.

Excerpts reprinted with permission from *Starting Points: Meeting the Needs of Our Youngest Children*, Carnegie Corporation of New York, © April 1994.

Excerpts from articles interviewing Dr. Sally Ward. *The Observer* 7/17/93 "TV and hi-fi noise blamed for child speech problems" and from *The Guardian* 9/21/94 "Turn off, talk up" both by Andrew Hobbs. Reprinted with permission of Dr. Sally Ward.

This book was truly made possible by the incredible support, dedication, enthusiasm and persistence of my husband Robert. In all aspects of its creation he played a major role. His continual and unwavering involvement was an inspiration as well as a profound act of love and affection.

I am also deeply indebted to Dr. John Bowlby who developed attachment theory. While studying with him at Tavistock, in 1982, I was impressed by his deep respect for childhood experiences and their effects on behavior. I was also excited by his understanding of the need for proximity of attachment figures when under stress, the pain and anxiety associated with separation and the significance of loss at every age. Over the years, my own clinical observations are best explained by Dr. Bowlby's theoretical framework.

In addition, I feel grateful to the Los Angeles Bowlby Study Group, Drs. Pat Sable, Barbara and Karl Pottharst, Diana Taylor, and Robin Davis, for their support and for increasing my understanding of attachment theory.

A special thanks to Dr. Paulita Neal for initially urging me to write and begin the process of organizing my ideas on paper. I also want to thank Bernice Kert for acting as mentor as I entered the unfamiliar world of writing for publication. Her suggestions and advice were most helpful. Norman Lobsenz was invaluable. He turned around many a sentence and phrase to make the book more readable and concise.

Thank you Jody Snyder, Carol Magid, and Ann Gorbitz. They had the difficult and onerous task of preparing draft after draft to create the proposal and the final manuscript.

I am grateful to my daughter Carolyn Reeser and my sister-in-law Peggy Cluster for their insightful suggestions and critical comments.

I feel a deep sense of appreciation to Grace Freedson who had the faith and courage to accept my controversial book for publication. My thanks to Michael Tuller for his help and cooperation in the editing process.

As a child, I was indeed fortunate to have a mother and father who created for me a secure, predictable and intellectually stimulating home environment. They gave me the gifts of their love for which I am grateful.

Finally, my own children, Michael, James and Carolyn, provide me with overwhelming joy and inspiration as I watch them as parents "be there" for their own children.

Isabelle Fox

Contents

4 What Happens When Caregivers Change: The Dangers of "Caregiver Roulette"   60

5 Parental Versus Substitute Care: A Comparison   85

6 Why Parental Care is Worth It   96

7 Solutions:
How to Provide Continuity of Quality Care   139

8 Final Thoughts on "Being There"   181

Preface

During the past few years, few issues have generated more heated debate and emotional response than the subject of this book. *Being There: The Benefits of a Stay-At-Home Parent* deals with the dilemma many new and expectant parents face when considering who will care for their infant, toddler, or young child.

This book is written mainly for those parents who are, or can be, in a financial position to make some choices involving child care. It attempts to help those mothers and fathers appreciate the value of their presence in the lives of their children, and the profound importance of continuity of care in the first preverbal years, particularly for parents who feel they must work full-time. Furthermore, the book explores how each parent can play an essential role in discipline, cognitive function, language development, and the teaching of social and moral values.

I warn of the dangerous effects of "caregiver roulette." This term describes the pervasive use of frequently changing caregivers that is now endemic to millions of young children. Usually, when both mother and father are employed full-time, 80 percent of the child's waking hours are spent with substitute caregivers. Unfortunately, these caregivers change with disturbing frequency, often every four or five months. I explain how such discontinuity of care is emotionally devastating, with life-long negative results, because it affects the ability of children to trust their important primary caregivers. This in turn affects their ability to relate to others, to learn, to develop an optimistic approach to life, and even to abide by the rules of society.

The many problems relating to changing caregivers seem to be overlooked probably because their consequences often do not show up until years later. Only recently have we begun to realize that children can experience serious emotional reactions to this "loss" during infancy.

It is also clear that this message concerning the importance of continuity of quality care is disturbing and, for many, guilt producing. As a result, parents may reject the conclusion that frequent changes in caregivers can have long-range effects. It is understandable that many may grow angry at the message, and look elsewhere for comfort.

I realize that some mothers and fathers may be hostile, rejecting, or nonresponsive to their own children. It is also true that many substitute caregivers can provide a nurturing environment in which infants and toddlers thrive. However, this book addresses the majority of mothers and fathers, who do have the emotional health and motivation to become involved and loving caregivers to their children.

I want to emphasize my own commitment to the idea that career fulfillment is just as important for women to achieve as for men. I have no wish to raise a regressive voice in the struggle of women to further their professional goals and ambitions and to enhance their economic power base. Nor do I care to be a part of any "backlash" against the feminist movement. Rather, my aim in writing this book is to shift the focus to the needs of our infants and toddlers and other young children as well as attempting to raise the consciousness and status of parenting so that both mothers and fathers grow to respect and appreciate this role.

One of today's difficulties is that many young people are programmed to feel they can have all aspects of the "good life" at the same time. In other words, they feel they should be able to simultaneously experience the joys of parenthood, the stimulation and ego gratification of a career, and the increased material benefits of two incomes, and to do justice to all of these goals. Actually, it is possible to achieve all these goals in a lifetime, but not concurrently if young children are to be considered.

My position is that one parent, either mother or father, should act as primary caregiver at least during the child's preverbal years. This is approximately the first two or three years of life. During this time, a parent may find it necessary to put his or her career "on hold" while parenthood temporarily takes precedence. During this brief part of the child's life, parents who provide positive and responsive parenting make a valuable investment in the future of their child, their family, and society. It is an investment that has the potential to pay large dividends to all in the years to come.

I have enormous sympathy for today's parents who are confronted with many economic, social, and media pressures that past generations have been spared. But, I was motivated to write this book for the sake of our young children who are often the victims of today's parental choices.

These young children, who cannot speak for themselves, have few support groups. They have few advocates or spokespersons to plead their cause. They cannot "pressure" or plead for quality and continuity of care with money, votes, or energy. They are too young and too powerless.

Therefore, this book attempts to speak for these young children, while recognizing the difficult dilemma their parents face today.

My book has four central goals:

1. **To impart an understanding of basic attachment theory.** Attachment theory explains how we become secure, first as children and later as adults. The English psychiatrist, John Bowlby, was one of the first authorities to observe and describe the significance of early bonding between infants and their mothers and to develop attachment theory to explain behavior. The theory explains that the infant feels most secure when it is in close proximity to the person who cares for him or her. This "attachment" between the newborn infant and the caregiver begins to form very early in the infant's life, as he or she is nurtured during the hundreds of interactions necessary for survival. Slowly, the infant learns that a particular caregiver provides a predictable, safe, and comfortable world for the infant. An attachment begins to form and grow with this caregiver who is constantly

available to the baby. It is with and because of this person that the very young child develops a secure base from which he or she feels free to explore their world.

I explain how stranger anxiety and separation anxiety is a normal part of the infant's development, how children become "securely attached," "anxiously attached," or "detached." Furthermore, my book discusses how infants and toddlers create "working models," which are expectations of how they will be treated in the future. The reaction of children to loss and separation are also described.

2. **To show the advantages—to both the child and the family—of parental involvement in the childrearing process throughout the childhood years.** Parents can play a very important part in the cognitive, emotional, and social development of their children. While substitute caregivers may offer adequate care, motivated parents will usually be able to provide a far richer and more nurturing social and intellectual environment for their children. Such parental involvement is of great value in the early preverbal years as well as the later years of childhood. Generally, the parent will be more willing and enthusiastic in protecting, holding, cuddling, comforting, feeding, playing with, stimulating, and communicating with their infant and toddler. And, as the child grows and matures, both in the preschool and school years, parents are also generally better able to stimulate, educate, and protect the child and enrich his or her life. Parents play an important role in language development, in discipline, in communicating moral and social values, in providing enriched play environments, and in the creation of family rituals and traditions for the family.

3. **To explain how "caregiver roulette," or frequently changing caregivers for infants and toddlers, can cause profound emotional damage as bonds and attachments are disrupted and how these events can produce long-range and even lifetime problems.**

Researchers have confirmed that many children who experience discontinuity of early primary caregivers, and who therefore do not develop secure attachments, are at a much increased risk for the development of problems that increasingly plague our society. These include:

- inability to learn a moral code and obey our laws;
- inability to successfully learn from teachers and traverse our educational system;
- inability to resist the temptations of drugs, alcohol, and substance abuse;
- inability to form and sustain intimate relations and consequent problems in getting and staying married;
- increased susceptibility to serious mental illness such as depression.

4. **To provide solutions and practical approaches for all families in providing continuity of care for young children.** I explain how all parents can take steps to provide continuity of child care. These suggestions cover single parents as well as parents in "nuclear" families. They cover families with minimal incomes as well as families with ample incomes and assets. They include:

- a description of the many different methods by which parents with varying incomes can find substitute caregivers who could provide the needed continuity and thus help to avoid disruptions caused by changing caregivers;
- alternative arrangements that will allow parents themselves to more fully participate in the childrearing process. For those parents whose finances are tight, but who nevertheless wish to care for their own children, suggestions are made that will help parents to achieve these goals utilizing their creativity and motivation.

My book acknowledges that the grave social problems I describe are not entirely caused by frequently changing care-

givers in the preverbal lives of our children. Of course, there
are other causes. However, there is a growing body of clinical
evidence to show that frequent losses and separations involving primary caregivers are factors that have a profound
impact on a child's future, and that poor attachment experiences are one of the significant causes of long-range problems for children. These concerns have been voiced by many
prominent authorities in the mental health community, such
as John Bowlby, T. Berry Brazelton, Alan Sroufe, Jay Belsky,
Mary Ainsworth, Mary Main, Selma Fraiberg, Ken Magid,
Penelope Leach, and others.

It is my concern that many parents in the 1990s are not
aware of the existence or the significance of caregiver
roulette. Nor are they aware of the profound benefits provided by a stay-at-home parent.

There is another less obvious and less discussed benefit
from parental presence. Whether or not both parents work
away from home, accidents can happen to infants and toddlers. Also, we know that angers can flare, negative care can
occur, and children can be frightened. But at least parents
who are at home know of these events and have the opportunity to take their child to a doctor if sick or injured, or to otherwise demonstrate concern and affection. Thus, they can
more immediately and appropriately respond as loving parents to their child.

It is my sincere hope and intent to encourage both expectant and new parents to make whatever temporary sacrifices
and adjustments are required in order that they can be there
for our youngest citizens during their most vulnerable and
formative years.

We all know that seeds are more likely to flower abun-
dantly and bear delicious fruit if they are planted in fertile
soil, watered regularly, and nourished with plenty of sunshine. Children are no different.

Who Cares for Our Children:
A Parent's Dilemma

I t is morning. Helen wakes, stretches, and turns over in bed to give her husband a good-morning kiss. To her surprise he isn't there. She hears footsteps entering the room, turns again, and is startled to see a stranger coming toward her—someone whose face and voice are unfamiliar. The stranger bends down, arms out-stretched, and begins to lift Helen from her bed. The stranger's touch is frightening. Helen starts to cry out—and then, abruptly, awakens to the light of day.

Helen has had a bad dream. Before too long, its disquieting emotional echoes will fade away. But for millions of infants and toddlers, Helen's bad dream is all too often a reality—a reality that is repeated many times during their first few years of life.

Each day, millions of American infants and toddlers face a terrifying trauma of which few parents are aware.

Consider the feelings of fright and helplessness in an infant who cannot talk or understand words, who cannot protect himself or herself against the approach of a stranger—a new caregiver whose voice, looks, smell, and touch are unfamiliar. Suddenly, with no explanation nor the ability to understand one, the child is confronted with a completely different person in place of the mother or other familiar caregiver

1

with whom the child was beginning to develop an all-important bond and attachment.

This experience, which confronts increasing numbers of middle-class infants and toddlers, is a phenomenon that has developed in the last two decades. It is a result of multiple pressures that the average middle-class family did not face in years past. Dual family incomes are now increasingly built into the family budget. In addition to this, middle-class women in the 1990s have acquired career expectations that may be in conflict with the role of mother.

Many careers outside the home provide intellectual stimulation and ego satisfaction, as well as comfortable augmentation of the family income. A wife who earns a significant income, or is building a significant career, often feels a sense of value and fulfillment that she is reluctant to forego, even temporarily.

We should not be surprised, then, by the steady exodus of mothers from home to workplace. Typically, a mother today returns to work when her infant is less than six months old, leaving the child in substitute care either in a home setting or at a day-care facility. The reasons for use of such substitute care are usually economic. Parents often state that "we need two incomes to pay our bills. And we have arranged for a wonderful sitter to care for our baby."

There is a widely accepted perception that any reasonably responsible person can properly diaper, feed, bathe, and generally care for a preverbal infant.

Is it true that "anyone" can care for a baby?

Furthermore, women with a high degree of specialized training and education (such as lawyers, doctors, teachers, writers, editors) often feel they would be wasting their abilities and training if they continued to carry out the mundane routines of daily infant care. There is also a general perception that substitute care is "just fine," so long as the caregiver is responsible, not abusive, and keeps the child safe, clean, and fed.

These generally accepted concepts provide a sense of comfort, and a source of reduced guilt and anxiety, for the millions of parents who go to work each day and leave their infants—for most of the child's waking hours—with substitute caregivers. And these comforting, generally accepted concepts would be valid *if* the substitute caregiver were not only nurturing and competent, but also provided *continuity* of such care throughout the preverbal years.

The Carnegie Corporation, a highly respected institution studied the first three years of life in its landmark 1994 publication *Starting Points: Meeting the Needs of Our Youngest Children.*[1] The report describes the advantages of child-rearing by a few "dependable adults" who provide "a secure base from *Continuity of positive and nurturing care is—today—increasingly denied to our young children with unfortunate consequences.* which the infant can explore the larger, social and physical world."[2] The report further explains that "for healthy development, infants and toddlers need a continuing relationship with a few caring people, beginning with their parents and later including other childcare providers. If this contact is substantial and consistent, young children can form trusting attachments that are needed for healthy development throughout life."[3]

But sadly, continuity of care is today increasingly being denied to most American infants. Primary caregivers for pre-verbal infants, whether at home or in a day-care center, come and go with unfortunate frequency. The rate of turnover, as we shall see, is phenomenal.

Moreover, few of us are aware of the long-term implications of these frequent changes. Infants cannot be prepared for these changes because they lack the ability to understand words until they are about two years old. But by that age, the constant change of primary caregivers has already been experienced by the child as a profound emotional loss. This sense of loss extends its negative influence over the child's development for decades to come.

Objectives of This Book

FIRST - To describe and illustrate the problems that can arise from the lack of continuity of infant and toddler care, and to emphasize the importance of a parent "being there" in those early years to provide such continuity.

SECOND - To explore and discuss how parents are (usually) more motivated than substitutes to provide both cognitive stimulation and emotional support for their children at all ages, although the primary focus of this book is on the young child.

THIRD - To offer specific solutions that can ensure continuity of quality care for preverbal children and establish quality care for older ones, even if both parents are employed.

What "Continuity" is and Why it is So Essential to the Formation of "Secure Attachment"

By "continuity" I mean the predictable presence of the *primary* caregiver. This is the person who cares for an infant during most of his or her waking hours and with whom the infant forms an "attachment" or "bond." Some authorities refer to "continuity" as "consistency of care."

> *"Continuity" means the predictable presence of the primary caregiver.*

The best way to understand the emotional impact of terms such as "continuity," "consistency," "predictable presence," and "secure attachment"—and the lack thereof—is to imagine how the infant reacts when caregivers come and go. Consider the example of a two-year-old child we will call "Timmy," whose mother returns to full-time employment when he is four months old. Timmy's experience is typical of many children I have treated in my practice as a psychotherapist. From his history, we can infer some of his feelings, random thoughts, and responses, and through them we can more effectively understand the stresses produced by frequent changes in caregivers. We know Timmy cannot put his feelings into words, but let us take that leap and infer what he is thinking so we can better understand what he is experiencing.

TIMMY'S STORY

When I was born, I cried to be close to my mommy, to hear her heartbeat, to smell her body. I liked to nurse because it gave me some of the same pleasure I felt when I was growing inside her. During those first months I was getting used to my mommy rocking me, changing my diapers, smiling down at me, making enjoyable sounds. I knew the way she smelled and talked. I liked the way she smelled, held me in her arms, and the way she hugged me and carried me around. I never had to cry too long. Either my mommy or daddy would come and try to make me feel better. I felt I was a wanted, loved, and protected baby.

One day when I was about four months old and beginning to trust the way things would go during my day, my mommy went back to work. Betty, a new lady, came to give me my bottle, hold me, and diaper me. I did not like it at all. Why did my mommy go away? I cried a lot to try to get my mommy or daddy back to take care of me. I cried longer and harder than I ever did before.

After a long, long time, my mommy *did* come home. I was glad to see her, but she left again the next day. I guess I just wasn't so special to her anymore.

After a week or so I got used to Betty, although I was still angry that my mommy wasn't there. Betty kept me clean and fed. She did not laugh or talk to me as much as my mommy and daddy did. But Betty did have a few good songs. After a while I got used to her smell, and her voice. She was cheerful. She picked me up and held me when I was sad, just like my mom did when she took care of me all day long.

When I was about eight months old, Betty suddenly disappeared. I don't know why she did not come anymore. Now someone named Agatha took care of me. I was mad and sad, both at the same time. Not only didn't I see mommy when I wanted her, but I didn't have Betty either. And this was just when I'd gotten to like her.

Why did she leave? Nobody could tell me. She just left. I guess I am not too lovable. Nobody wants to stay with me.

I did not like Agatha. She had a different odor. She didn't hold me the way that Betty did and she was grouchy when my mom wasn't around. I was so sad I slept a lot. I did not feel like crawling around or trying to stand up. I would cry, but that did not bring my mommy home any sooner. At night I would wake up a few times to see if my mom or dad were really there. Mom would get mad at me, but I didn't care. I was mad too.

When I was almost a year old, Agatha stopped coming. She gave up on me, too. My mommy drove me every morning to a strange house where a lady named Jenny and a woman who helped her took care of me, another baby, a four-year-old girl, and twin boys two years old. There were lots of toys but I was too scared and worried to play.

Jenny smiled a lot and told my mommy I'd get along fine with the other kids. My mom kissed me, said "I'll be back later," and left. I cried and cried. Jenny tried to comfort me but then the other baby started to wail and she had to hand me over to someone else while she fed the other baby. This second woman told me in a mean voice to stop crying, but I couldn't. I wanted my crib, my own blanket, my own room. I wanted my mommy or daddy.

When my mommy finally came to pick me up, I couldn't tell her about the lady with the mean voice. When Jenny told my mommy that I was "fine" I couldn't tell her I had cried and didn't eat almost all day. In the weeks that followed I could not tell my mom about the four-year-old who pushed me off a chair so I hurt my head. I really needed my mommy then. I could not tell her how the twins grabbed toys from me, or that no grown-up played with us, or smiled, or talked to us, unless another parent came to visit.

The longer I stay at Jenny's house, the more I feel no one loves me. My mommy hugs me and *says* she loves me. But if she really loved me, she would not leave me most of the time, and would be there when I get hurt or sad. I guess I am not important anymore because she spends most of her time and energy at her office.

When she picks me up and takes me home late in the day, she is rushed and tired. She and my daddy are grumpy. When they read to me they want me to go to sleep right away. I hear them tell their friends about the "quality time" they spend with me when they get home from work. I wish I had more of my mommy during the day, and less of this "quality time." Then I would be able to depend on her, trust her, and feel that I am special to her. I would be able to worry less.

Now that I am almost two years old, I am so upset and angry with my mommy and daddy that I do not like listening to them because they do not listen to what I need. I guess I am going to have to rely on myself for comfort and for pleasure. Crying does not change anything around here, so I will just stop crying, and stop protesting. I will suck my thumb more and maybe find more toys to throw around.

I hear my parents tell their friends how guilty they feel about leaving me at Jenny's place, but how they really need two incomes because they want to move to a bigger house and buy a new car. I like the home and the car we have now. I wish my mommy and daddy knew that the only thing I care about is having them with me. But my needs do not seem to be important to them so I guess they will just keep leaving me with Jenny, or someone like her, for a long, long time.

Let us step back and take a closer look at what really happened to Timmy during his first eighteen months of life. Remember: what happened to him is being increasingly repeated in millions of American homes.

Timmy "told" us how comfortable and secure he felt during the first four months of life when his mom and dad took care of him—rocking him, changing his diapers, smiling, and responding quickly if he cried. He knew his mom's smell, voice, and other physical characteristics (reminiscent of *Diary of a Baby*, by Dr. Daniel Stern).[4]

Then, at the tender age of four months, this blissful routine was abruptly shattered. Mom returned to work and a new primary caregiver took over during 80 percent or more of Timmy's waking life. Does this percentage seem shocking? Perhaps, but the fact is that a caregiver who is with an infant from 8:00 A.M. to 6:00 P.M. five days a week is responsible for the great bulk of the child's waking life!

This disruption of continuity, and of the fragile, not yet fully developed attachment and bond, was a powerful blow to Timmy's emotional stability. Contributing to the trauma was the fact that Timmy lacked language; there was no way his mom could prepare Timmy for the change in caregivers. To quote the noted British psychologist and child expert, Dr. Penelope Leach, a child of Timmy's age "has no way of knowing that the parent who left him will come back, no way of measuring the passage of time, not even any way of retaining the parent's image in mind so as to anticipate her return."[5]

Infants and toddlers can suffer when primary caregivers change.

Nevertheless, like many infants, Timmy was resilient. After a time he had begun to trust Betty, his first substitute caregiver, and to establish a bond with her. Again, his life became comfortable and predictable since he had a nurturing and compassionate caregiver who met his needs.

But then, four months later, when Timmy was only eight months old, he was confronted with another upheaval when Betty abruptly quit and he was relegated to a new primary caregiver—Agatha. To compound this emotional assault, a few months later Agatha disappeared and Jenny, with her unfamiliar home with other children, entered Timmy's life.

Describing the feelings of a child like Timmy "deserted" by many caregivers, Dr. Leach agrees: "The despair of the baby who feels deserted is real despair, even though the desertion is no more than a parent's routine departure for work."[6] And, of course Timmy's problem was far more extreme since he "lost" one primary caregiver after another. More clearly than reams of text, the recounting of Timmy's sad experience portrays the trauma caused by a lack of continuity of positive care, and by abrupt and repeated changes of caregivers in the preverbal years.

Unfortunately, when a child like Timmy is brought to a therapist as a preschooler or school-age child, little in the way of early history is available to the therapist. The working mother or father is often not aware of significant events that occurred during these early years. Was Timmy frightened by a dog? Did he fall off a bed? Did he have to cry and cry until he was given his bottle? Did a child push him over?

Working parents are often not aware of significant events in their child's life.

Timmy cannot tell the therapist that Agnes was depressed and irritable, cannot tell of his sadness when Betty abruptly departed, or of his fears at being left in a strange day-care setting. These early events are almost always impossible to retrieve. The child's memories are not accessible to aid the therapeutic process. A lack of historical information from either the patient or the patient's parents as well as Timmy's inability to rely on adults makes him a poor candidate for therapeutic intervention. Thus, the child is left with wounds that are difficult to treat and may never heal. These unresolved preverbal experiences may seriously impair Timmy's ability to function in the world and to reach his intellectual potential.

For therapy to become a truly reparative experience it is important to be able to form a relationship with a therapist that is initially based upon trust. But the ability to trust depends on the quality of a child's first experiences with his or her caregivers. In Timmy's case, he never formed a close and secure attachment to anyone and so would likely be wary of forming a close relationship with a therapist.

It has been my clinical experience in working with young children over the past 35 years that the problems brought to my office in the last decade are much more severe than those 15 to 30 years ago. Other child therapists agree that they are not treating simple developmental or neurotic issues today but more difficult problems dealing with ability to form relationships, hyperactivity, and extremes in aggression. These have replaced more treatable complaints such as sibling rivalry, toilet training, bed-wetting, parent/child power struggles, eating problems, and so on.

These subtle shifts in the severity of children's dysfunctions seem to have slowly evolved. Histories also reveal that more and more of these children were cared for by many different substitutes early in their lives. It seemed to indicate that there was a causative relationship between early discontinuity of care and the severity of the problems I was treating.

The Choice: Parent or Substitute

All parents make caregiving choices for their children. The choice should be one of two alternatives:

1. That a parent (or parents) stay at home and provide the all-important continuity that was denied to Timmy. Clearly, this alternative is not feasible for *all* parents, but it is certainly possible for *many* millions of parents if they are willing to make the temporary financial and career sacrifices that may be required. (See Chapter 2.) Of course this also depends upon the asset/income

status of the parents and what practical steps they can take to implement their decision (see Chapter 7).

> **What are the caregiving choices that every parent must make?**

2. The second alternative is to take the necessary steps to find a substitute caregiver who can offer the *continuity* of positive nurturing care young children need in order to achieve their intellectual and emotional potential, and to have a fulfilling life. (See Chapter 7 for ways to assure continuity of care by a substitute.)

Later in this book we will explore both the benefits of choice number one, as well as practical methods of implementing the second choice. But, whichever is selected, a successful effort to provide continuity of responsive care will produce these important rewards for the child:

- a sense of optimism and self-esteem;
- an increased ability to listen to and to learn from parents, teachers, and other adults;
- the ability to internalize the positive moral values of parents and community; and
- the ability to form intimate relationships in adolescence and in adulthood. In practical terms, this means a greater probability of happy and enduring marriages.

Parents may ask, "Even though my infant or toddler lacked continuity of caregiving, why can't he or she be provided with such continuity at ages 3, 4, or 5, for example, and develop the secure attachment at that later age?" The answer is that while predictability and stability of care is always of value at any age, *the ability to trust is established mainly in the preverbal years.* It is the primary developmental task in infancy. It is during these years that the child has his or her first experiences with relationships. If trust is *not* formed during *this* period, powerful unconscious defenses are created to protect oneself against the pain of disappointment, abandonment, and loss. These defenses serve as an emotional armor. But the downside is that they also "arm" the child against forming the type of intimate

> *The ability to trust is the primary developmental task in the preverbal years (birth to age 2 or 3).*

alliances so essential to the creation of positive relationships. Moreover, there is compelling and convincing recent evidence that these defenses remain as part of the child's basic character structure throughout his or her life.

As L. Alan Sroufe stated, "early experience may have special significance because it provides a foundation for all later development. Poor quality care in the early years, when first attachment relationships are forming, may have more profound effects than equally poor care later."[7]

It is extremely difficult to assess the positives or negatives of substitute care when a parent is not there to observe, evaluate, or question. How do we know what quality of care the infant is receiving? How gently, how joyfully, how quickly, how attuned, and how empathetic are the caregiver's responses to the needs of a vulnerable infant and toddler?

Theoretical Background of Attachment Theory

The theoretical foundation that enables us to identify the problems in developing secure attachments in preverbal children was described, beginning in the 1940s, by the British psychiatrist John Bowlby. He, along with psychologist Mary Ainsworth, was among the first to observe and describe the bonding between infants and their mothers, the concept of "secure base," and the reaction to mother-child separations that was illustrated in Timmy's story.

Bowlby noticed early in his studies that children separated from their parents during the massive bombing raids on London in World War II (they were sent for safety to homes in the countryside) were more emotionally damaged than children who stayed with their mothers during the attacks. In a paper entitled "Forty-Four Juvenile Thieves,"[8] Bowlby reported the high proportion of delinquent boys who had suffered early maternal separation.

From clinical observations, Bowlby began to formulate what is known as "attachment theory." Its basic precept is that an infant instinctively behaves in many ways that serve to maintain close proximity to the mother or other primary caregiver. He found that infants and young children separated from the mother or mother

Bowlby states that infants behave in ways to promote proximity to primary caregivers.

figure suffer severe emotional distress. Unlike Freud, who emphasized instinctual drives (sex, aggression, fantasies, and internal conflicts) as motivators of behavior, Bowlby was far more concerned with children's "real" experiences, and with the quality of their relationship with their parents or primary caregivers. It is interesting that a half century later this view is supported by the Carnegie Report: "By the end of the first year, infants have a reasonable memory of important major events that have special meaning for them."[9]

Another tenet of Bowlby's theory is the importance of the infant's bond with its earliest caregiver, and the profound effect early childhood events associated with this bonding—or lack of it—have on later life. "The secure personal base," Bowlby writes, "from which a child, an adolescent, or an adult goes out to explore and to which he returns from time to time, is one I have come to regard as crucial for an understanding of how an emotionally stable person develops and functions all through his life."[10] Bowlby believes that the primary "attachment" between caregiver and child serves as a prototype for later social relationships; thus the *early* lack of positive caregiving causes *later* social consequences. Many developmental psychologists agree that children require sensitive, responsive, and consistent care. Infants have to be not only protected and fed but stimulated and loved. As Dr. R. A. Spitz noticed when observing institutionalized children, if physical care is all that is given, many fail to thrive and often die.[11]

Early in the 1970s, animal researchers Suomi and Harlow studied the effects of maternal separation on monkeys. They found that monkeys had similar problems when denied normal maternal care. These isolated infant animals, for example, displayed severe emotional distress and exhibited bizarre behavior even though they had food, water, and so on. Their abnormal behavior was strikingly similar to that exhibited by the institutionalized children described by Dr. Spitz.[12]

Why the Problems Created by Constant Changes of Caregivers Have Been Ignored

There is little doubt that problems of the earliest childhood years have been largely ignored by the public, government agencies, and the mental health community. This is one of the primary reasons why the Carnegie Corporation elected to focus on this period of children's lives: "From the prenatal period to age 3, this judgment," says the Report, "reflected the fact that this age period is perhaps the most neglected."[13] To highlight the large number of children affected, the Report also pointed out that there are "12 million children under the age of 3 in the United States today."[14]

Non-responsive caregiving and childhood stress have often been ignored by both the public and the mental health community.

There are several logical reasons why parents—and most segments of the mental health community—have for so long and to such a great extent ignored the problems of changing caregivers, and the consequences of discontinuity of care as it affects children.

The first reason is that the problem has crept up upon us slowly and quietly. No trumpets sounded a warning as, year after year, more and more women left the home and entered the workplace. (Or, if there *were* trumpets, they were blown to celebrate this societal change!) As late as 1965 only 17 percent of the mothers of one-year olds worked full- or part-time.[15] Thus, these "at home" mothers provided continuity of care without anyone thinking about it, unless a parent died or was divorced.

Since then, we have lived through a silent social revolution. A combination of economic pressures (some real and some stimulated by advertising), as well as the burgeoning feminist movement, resulted in a startling 180-degree turn in the statistics. Today well over 50 percent of all mothers—even those of very young children—work outside the home. But the entire about-face has been so gradual that few in the mental health community have taken note of its effect on young children.

A silent social revolution has profoundly affected our infants and toddlers.

The *consequences* of frequent changes of caregivers have also been largely unappreciated. They are discussed in detail in Chapter 4. They include delinquency, school dropouts, depression, substance abuse, and difficulties with intimacy. These problems may not be obvious until many years have passed. Thus, parents do not see—or accept—the causal connection between changing caregivers during *infancy* and toddlerhood, and negative behavior *years* later. They pay scant attention to the quality of their child's early attachments. Instead, parents tend to blame this negative behavior on schools, peers, television, and even the current caregivers.

Yet, as psychologist Jay Belsky noted when he commented upon the effects of placing infants in day care: "A relatively persuasive circumstantial case can be made that early infant care may be associated with increased avoidance of mother, possibly to the point of greater insecurity in the attachment relationship, and that such care may be associated with diminished compliance and cooperation with adults, increased aggressiveness and possibly even greater social maladjustment in the preschool and early school-age years."[16]

The second basic reason why the problems of changing caregivers have been ignored is simple: the message is unpleasant and disturbing.

The reason why problems of changing caregivers has been ignored: The "message" is disturbing.

No parent or expectant parent wants to feel that going to work and leaving an infant or toddler with a paid substitute will be harmful. And it is even more disturbing to contemplate the obvious and practical solution: that a parent make some financial adjustment or personal sacrifice in order to be able to stay home for two years or so, or until the infant can truly understand why mom and dad are away most of the time. It is easier to deny that the problem exists, and to "attack the messenger" as sexist, regressive, wrong, or "nonresponsive" to the realities of the day. Few of us want to admit that we have done anything to endanger our children.

Mental health professionals and parents are well aware of the long-range negative effects of *sexual* and *physical* abuse. But now, with this book, we hope to explore the concept that, for infants and toddlers, frequent changes in primary caregivers, and chaotic and unpredictable attachments, create a different and subtle form of emotional distress. So subtle is this distress that most of us do not realize it exists. But if we can recognize and understand what has occurred in recent years, and why it has occurred, we should be able to face the dilemma of who cares for our children with more sensitivity and insight. This book is dedicated to that goal. As parents come to understand the problems, they may find it more feasible to seek out and select solutions applicable to the care of their own children.

Throughout the book we will cite experiences that show how parents (as compared with nonparental substitutes) can enrich the lives of their children throughout *all* of the years of childhood. We recognize and discuss what should be obvious—that most parents are eager to provide affection, stimulation and accountability for their children. We show how a parental presence provides many "hidden" benefits at *every* stage of a child's life.

> **Parents are usually motivated to enrich the lives of their children at all ages.**

I realize that *some* mothers or fathers may be abusive, rejecting, or nonresponsive to their children, or miserably unhappy in their role of parent. And I recognize that many substitute caregivers *can* provide a nurturing and positive environment, one in which infants and toddlers can thrive. However, this book speaks mainly to that majority of mothers and fathers who have the emotional health and strength and motivation to become involved with and loving caregivers to their children.

Finally, I recognize that some of the suggestions I will make to encourage either a mother or father to act as primary caregiver may not be practical from an economic standpoint for many families. To these parents I also offer some realistic solutions (see Chapter 7) suggesting how they, too, can supply continuity of care in the early years of childhood using substitute care. I also discuss how part-time work can allow more time for the child to form an attachment to the parent and, at the same time, not become so emotionally dependent upon the substitute caregiver.

The focus of this book is on the child. It is written to help mothers and fathers better understand some of the emotional needs of their children. As I point out in the concluding chapter, there are few advocates for our nonverbal infants and toddlers. Indeed, they do need an advocate! I know it is not a "feel good" book for parents. I wish it could be. It does not massage our egos as parents and tell us what a great job we are doing despite imposing economic obstacles. Nor does it assuage our guilt when our children are confronted with many separations and losses.

And while I have attempted to be understanding of the problems parents and expectant parents face, I have felt for many years that it is our youngest citizens—our adults and leaders of tomorrow—who need a voice early in life, who need protection, support, and the ability to trust. But these children cannot articulate their need for continuity of care or for a mom or a dad to "be there."

Giving the Gift of Love:
Parenthood as a Temporary Career

E ver since human society reached that point in its march toward civilization when sheer survival was no longer the overriding daily concern, the search for reciprocal love has been the chief desire and major preoccupation of most men and women.

From time to time, pollsters ask Americans what they consider the most important ingredient in a recipe for personal happiness. More than nine out of ten people rank "love" at the top of the list, far ahead of money, status, power, and fame. But though the ability to give and accept love is so wished for, so sought after, and so important to our lives, it nevertheless seems—so much of the time for so many people—to escape our grasp. We do not need here to cite the evidence of divorce statistics, or to quote the disheartening observations of experts on the proliferation of dysfunctional relationships, to convince you of the unhappy fact that most people have trouble achieving intimacy, and in making an emotional commitment. In short, it seems that all too few of us have that ability that all of us want—to experience and sustain a loving relationship.

But suppose someone told you that you have it within your power, as a parent, to give your child a magic gift: the ability to love. Suppose, further, you were told that this magical gift would do even more than give your child the ability to give and accept love. Suppose you were told that this magic would also help to instill in your child other qualities, such as curiosity, creativity, energy, resilience, morality, motivation,

18

perseverance and self-esteem—qualities that will make for a happy and successful life, during both childhood and his or her adult years. Clearly, no parent would refuse this offer.

Of course, as with all magical gifts, a "price" is attached. You are told that the gift must be given each day for a few years. You are told it is up to you to provide the infant with the positive presence of a loving, joyful caregiver who is responsive and attuned to your young child's needs. You are also told to provide continuity of care with a minimum of losses and disruptions until the child is approximately two or three years of age. This span of time covers the preverbal period that ends (about age two for some children and up to age three for others) when the child can make himself or herself understood with reasonable fluency and can comprehend what others are saying and be better prepared for change.

If you wish to give your child the ability to love, a "price" must be paid.

This is no easy gift to provide even when a parent is present. But the gift of love is almost never possible when the child has little contact with his or her primary caregiver in the early formative years.

Importance of the Primary Caregiver

Imagine a spouse who verbally declares his love but is rarely home, works long hours during the week and spends much of each weekend with friends, and who is seldom available when needed for comfort and affection. It is easy to see how one could come to doubt the strength of this spouse's love and commitment. It is also clear that, over time, one's sense of trust in that person would erode.

Similarly, parental expressions of love for a young child cannot be simply verbal; an infant does not understand the words, "I love you." For the infant to have the sense of being loved, those words must be accompanied by—translated into, if you will—*scores of daily nurturing interactions between parent and child.* These ponderous technical words simply refer to the loving, caring actions parents (or other primary caregivers) perform for and with the child every day: giving a bottle or singing a lullaby, holding and rocking a fretsome child, cooing and talking baby talk, playing with a toy, or reading a picture book together.

If caregivers change frequently, the infant or toddler will be unable to develop the confidence that his or her world is safe and predictable. If the person to whom he or she is beginning to grow attached suddenly disappears and is replaced by an unfamiliar caregiver, it is as if an emotional rug has been suddenly pulled out from under the young child causing stress and anxiety. As a result, the child may have more difficulty forming a close affectionate bond with a future caregiver, and this may reduce his or her ability, throughout life, to form loving and intimate relationships.

Unfortunately, young children in today's America are increasingly likely to suffer frequent changes of primary caregivers. This is true whether there is a succession of nannies or housekeepers in the home, or the constant high turnover among staff members at even the "best" day-care centers.

To understand the feelings of an infant, when caregivers change, try to imagine how it feels to be a patient in a hospital setting. There are usually two or three daily shifts in the nursing staff over a 24-hour day. A strange nurse suddenly appears at the bedside. For most adult patients, this can create a feeling of disruption and disappointment when the expected nurse fails to arrive.

In many cases, a relationship begins to develop between patient and nurse, even during eight hours of care. When a new nurse is introduced, further effort must be expended by the patient to build a connection to the new caregiver. However, after many changes, the patient may give up trying to relate and stay quiet and withdrawn.

The infant who cannot (yet) speak is vulnerable to the consequences of changing primary caregivers.

We may assume these feelings are similar to those of an infant who has been accustomed to the familiar smell, arms, and voice of a known caregiver. When a strange caregiver appears, we should remember that the infant is far more vulnerable than the adult in our example. The infant cannot speak or understand language and has not yet matured to the point where he or she can even begin to comprehend such changes in the person who is most important: the primary caregiver.

The Advantages of a Parent as Primary Caregiver

If it is economically feasible, there are clear-cut advantages to having a parent as primary caregiver. Parents are more motivated, and thus more dependable and less likely to disappear, to quit, or to move to another city. Unlike a substitute caregiver, they will not take a sudden unplanned-for vacation, nor make lame excuses for failing to show up in the morning. Of all possible caregivers, parents are the most motivated to provide both continuity and quality care.

In 1994 Dr. Benjamin Spock considered the problems of parental care and substitutes for it. He explained how desirable it is for at least one of the parents (if not both) "to have plenty of time with infants and small children in the first two or three years, not simply to feed, clothe and keep them

> **Dr. Spock: Better if one parent stays home 2–3 years.**

clean, but to give them a sense of security and intimacy with the parents." He further recommended that "If the family's economic situation permits, it is better for one parent not to work outside the home during this period."[1]

Penelope Leach also discussed the value of a parental presence: "However much they may delegate to other caregivers and to educational institutions, parents and parent figures are crucial to every phase of this long human childhood, not least because it is individual parents who most passionately want to meet the needs of their children and passion is what is needed."[2]

If that is true, mothers and fathers need to rethink their priorities, to put them into a new and broader perspective that transforms parenthood into a temporary career choice. At first blush, two years of virtually full-time parenting may seem too long a period to qualify for the adjective "temporary." But since most young mothers and fathers today can anticipate a working life of 25 to 40 years or more, taking time out for the relatively brief span of two years still leaves sufficient time to grow professionally, to achieve personal satisfaction, and to build a financial safety net, if not security.

More important is the fact that two years away from the job early in one's working life may not have serious long-term adverse career effects for the parent. Margaret Thatcher, the former British prime minister, is a perfect example of a mother who put her career on hold, and stayed home with her children until they were in school. Then she returned to politics and resumed her successful career.[3]

Conversely, exposing an infant or toddler to frequent changes of caregivers *is* more likely to have negative consequences, as discussed in Chapter 4.

Perhaps it is time for parents to rethink, as well, the meaning of the word "career." Perhaps "parenthood," or "motherhood" or "fatherhood," is in itself worthy of "career" status, certainly for the limited number of years involved, and certainly when parents realize the impact such a career choice can have on their children. For if parents can find a way to make parenthood a full-time temporary career during a child's preverbal years, they can take satisfaction in knowing they are attempting to give their young child the gift of a secure emotional foundation.

With this foundation a child is more likely:

- *To learn to trust and love.* As a result, the child will be better able to make and maintain rewarding intimate relationships throughout life; to marry and have a better chance of staying married; and to be empowered to pass on to his or her children the same secure emotional base.

What are the benefits to your child of the gift of love?

- *To move successfully through our educational system.* The child will be more able to trust and learn from teachers, to face and overcome school problems, and to achieve the maximum potential his or her native abilities allow.
- *To learn and to internalize a positive moral code* that adheres to society's rules and obligations.
- *To avoid drug, alcohol, and substance abuse,* and the concomitant problems they cause.
- *And, finally, to avoid depression,* and other emotional problems that have roots in the early years. Depressive behavior is seen in infancy when a baby's secure emotional attachment has been threatened and he or she experienced disruptions in the bonding process. A period of mourning and depression follows these losses.

Full-time temporary parenthood does *not* mean you must never leave the house, never hire a baby-sitter, never take a short vacation. It does mean that for most of that time *you* will be your child's *primary* caregiver—the person he or she can count on to "be there" when he or she needs you most. It means *you* (the parent) will

> **Full-time temporary parenthood does not mean the parent is a full-time maid/housekeeper.**

be doing the important work of helping your child form that basic emotional bond that will be his or her source of strength throughout life. Being there in the years to follow will further insure supervision, support, and accountability, which is so important in the transmission of values and in the development of disciplined behavior.

Nor, finally, does full-time temporary parenthood mean you must also do all the work involved in running a household. Some mothers are willing or even delighted to be home with their child full-time, but are not as ready to shoulder the burden of all the homemaking duties. But why should full-time parenthood necessarily mean full-time housework? Just as career women and men hire assistants and secretaries to facilitate their professional tasks, so a career mother or father should not apologize about asking for help with household chores. Help from a spouse, partner, from in-laws or grandparents, from extended family relatives, from friends or neighbors, or from paid help if financially feasible—are all important psychological supports. Because nonworking mothers or fathers often feel guilty about not bringing home a paycheck, some feel they must do everything themselves. But the result is they suffer a build-up of stress and resentment that, in the long run, militates against the calm and loving environment so vital to enhancing the attachment bond.

As Child Matures, Parental Time Can Diminish

Parents need to remember, too, that as the child matures and develops verbal skills, the time demands on the parent lessen. The verbal youngster can effectively make his or her needs known, and report the day's experiences. The verbal child better understands and more easily tolerates brief separations while parents either work or are absent for other reasons.

While toddlers who live with a stay-at-home parent will certainly cry when the parent eventually does go back to work, when the child is two or three years old, the child could be realistically prepared for this event beforehand since at age two or three the child is old enough to understand and communicate.

However, no parent should feel that he or she must stay at home for two years or so to act as the primary caregiver. Millions of parents who would like to do so cannot. The financial resources simply are not there. But all parents, without exception, do have an important obligation—the obligation to do everything possible to provide continuity of quality care for their young children. This concern applies not only to individual caregivers but also to staff personnel at day-care centers. Parents are obliged to make every effort to guarantee that those who care for their children are trained, warm, and compassionate. Above all, parents must make every effort to see that changes in caregivers are held to a minimum. (Chapter 7 offers specific suggestions to help parents accomplish this objective.) These are obligations all parents can carry out if they try.

Of course, providing continuity of care in the early years does not by itself guarantee that a child will grow up to achieve the lifetime rewards that are made possible by a secure emotional foundation. Later events—physical or mental abuse, illness, accidents, parental divorce or death—can affect future development in severely adverse ways. However, there is a large and growing body of research about the importance of a secure

> *Although continuity of care in the preverbal years will not guarantee success for your child, the emotional base it can provide will be vital.*

emotional base in the first three years of life. In this book I quote many eminent authorities on this subject. They include John Bowlby, Mary Ainsworth, Burton White, Benjamin Spock, the Carnegie and University of Colorado reports, and others.

It is also true that parental supervision and involvement, in the afterschool hours throughout the childhood years, will add to and enrich the lives of children and help them to reach their potential as creative and courageous individuals.

Why Mothers Return to Work

Most mothers—well over 50 percent by the mid 1990s—go back to work sometime during their child's earliest years. There are many reasons for this decision. One frequently stated reason is a real or perceived need to supplement the family income. This is particularly true in our consumer-oriented culture, where the media has influenced our materialistic desires. Countering the notion that "women must work" and that "families need two incomes" are studies that would seem to negate these popular catchphrases. These surveys indicate that literally millions of women who work do so to support an elevated lifestyle, to afford luxuries, to "keep up with one's friends," or for reasons other than true economic necessity.

Health consultant Harriet Heath reported that "writers and polls have been reporting for several years that as high as 80 percent of women in paid employment would work outside the home, even if they did not have to do so, for financial reasons."[4] Similarly, psychologist Jay Belsky notes that "it needs to be recognized that there exist a good number of families that could manage to forego two incomes" during the child's first year because of "whatever risks might be associated with day care."[5]

Reasons that are often given for women returning to work include:

- to compensate for lost income due to divorce, death of a spouse, or similar economic problem confronting the family;
- a yearning for increased intellectual or emotional stimulation, which both men and women believe the workplace will provide;
- to maintain and hone professional skills and abilities that a woman developed and used before the birth of her children;
- to avoid losing job seniority or career status. Many working women postpone having children so they can win a promotion, or gain a supervisory position or other elevated status. Mothers may feel that these gains will be lost if they fail to return to work promptly after their infant is born.
- the steady denigration of the role of homemaker and mother in contemporary culture. Both genders place increasing value on career development and the importance of enhancing financial status. As a result, the "stay-at-home parent" has found this role less valued. Both financial and societal pressures, therefore, motivate the new mother to resume her career—to value her professional role and ability to earn money—in order to define her "sense of self." One of the pressures unique to contemporary middle-class women is that many have invested much time in college education and in their

professional careers. As a result, they have postponed marriage and motherhood in favor of financial and professional status.

Many of these women cannot imagine getting satisfaction from the more intangible rewards of parenting and may be concerned about the stress of social isolation. They may be less than enthusiastic about getting out of a warm bed to soothe a crying baby, or about pushing a toddler in a swing, or singing or reading to a 14-month-old. These activities may lack the appeal offered by a "real job," and by the benefits that a job provides. Therefore, a paycheck at the end of the month may seem much more emotionally and intellectually fulfilling compared with feeding their child five or six times a day. So it is understandable that many of today's mothers face a fundamental emotional conflict over who will care for their infant and toddler.

- lastly, the real problem may be that many contemporary mothers are simply *unaware* of both the negative consequences of unreliable substitute childcare, and the real advantages that accrue to children if a parent—mother or father—is "there" for them not only on hurried evenings and weekends, but *all week long.*

> *Many parents are unaware of the negative consequences of unreliable substitute care.*

Single Parenthood: By Circumstance or by Choice

At present, it is becoming increasingly more frequent for both single men and women to opt for parenthood without establishing a reliable support system, spouse, partner, or committed family member.

While the desire for parenting may be understandable from the point

> *In single parenthood by choice, the best interests of the child are rarely considered.*

of view of the adult seeking fulfillment, the best interests of the child must be considered.

Single parenting makes the provision of continuity of care as well as other kinds of enriching and stimulating experiences far more difficult to provide. The single parent must earn a living. In most cases, this takes the parent away from the home. But this parent also needs to build a secure attachment to the child; yet the sorely needed support system for such a parent is usually difficult to provide.

Even though rewarding, the acts of nurturing and being responsive to children are exhausting. It is no mystery why teachers are given extended vacations to replenish their energy and enthusiasm for working daily with their students. Grandparents are often the first to admit that as much as they love their grandchildren, taking care of them is hard work. Generally they report how pleased they are to return them to their parents at the end of a visit.

Unfortunately, many parents become the sole support of their infant through death, divorce, or desertion by a mate. Though they did not necessarily choose single parenting, they are confronted with real stresses associated with their new roles.

Whatever the cause of the single parent family, the provision of continuity of care remains critical. If the parent can find a way to provide such continuity, either personally or by nurturing substitutes, they will have taken an important step in providing the gift of love.

The "Myth" of Quality Time

Many young working mothers I spoke with while researching this book raised the issue of "quality time." "Can't a bond and a secure attachment be formed and made strong by giving my child special attention during the time *I am* home?" they asked. One mother said she felt she was a much better parent *because* she worked outside the home. "If I were home all day with my baby and my two-year-old, with no other adults around to talk to, I think I'd go crazy," she said. "But at work I feel challenged and stimulated, so when I get home

I'm ready to give quality time to the children. I feel that quality time is more important than quantity time."

Many parents agree with this view. They tell me how they compensate for their absence during the workweek by concentrating on the children in the evenings, on weekends, and during vacation days. What they say sounds logical and convincing, and to some degree they are right: these moments of "quality time"—when a child is played with, listened to, read a story, taken on a neighborhood trip—are exquisitely valuable and not to be underestimated. They do comprise an important part of the developing bond with the parent, and *are* an integral factor in the growth of the child's sense of self.

But—and it is a large "but"—providing this kind of quality time is not as easy as we like to think it is. And, in many cases, it does not achieve its goals.

How much "quality time" is really available when parents work full-time?

The reality of the matter is that parents have many demands made on their time and energy. The job is only one commitment; most parents also have responsibilities to their community, their church, their friends and family, and perhaps to older children who are already in school. How much time can be available for "quality time?"

But let us say parents *have* held non-work-related commitments to a minimum. Even so, when both come home from work they are likely to be tired, harried, and eager to relax or talk to each other. The reality is that at the end of the day or week, working parents are likely to need nurturing themselves. As a result a child is often rushed through meal and bedtime rituals, and is deprived of quality time even at the very moment when it is supposed to be taking place.

At day's end the child, too, is likely to be tired, irritable, demanding; he or she may feel angry at the parents for being away all day. And if the child has started to form a bond (in the parents' absence) with the substitute caregiver, the child may be upset when the caregiver abruptly leaves. Result: neither parents nor child are able to mobilize the good feelings and relaxed atmosphere so necessary to create "quality time."

Dr. Penelope Leach also emphasizes the fallacy of the "quality time" concept: "The younger the child, the more impossible it is to schedule togetherness time," she writes. "You cannot make a tired baby stay awake for a day's worth of cuddling, and trying may be a selfish attempt to salve adult consciences and conflicts at the expense of overstimulated infants. You cannot easily persuade a one year old who wanted you to play with him this morning to take his one and only chance to play right now; if he is angry at your desertion, he will not let you off the hook that easily. And if you are not there when your toddler's first rhyme is spoken, you will not hear it or see her face as she hears what she has made. Magic moments happen when they happen and the painful truth is that the ones that are missed are gone forever."[6]

On weekends, personal and family chores have no doubt piled up. All too often infants and toddlers are expected to "tag along" while parents run these errands. Such expeditions are often not only not child-centered; they wind up being stressful both for parents and child. Trips to the grocery store, gas station, or the cleaners certainly cannot be counted as quality time spent with one's child; nor are household tasks—cooking, cleaning, doing laundry—usually a source of mutual pleasure or accomplishment. Of course, there are times when these outings or activities can prove interesting and the shared time together can provide the child with experiences into the adult world.

Yet when all is said and done many parents, if not most, reluctantly admit how little joyful time they *do* spend with their young children. The bottom line is that when both parents work full-time, quality time after work can be more a mythical concept than an experienced reality. Children thrive on "quantity time"—because its greater span of hours allows room for many more moments of true quality time. Dr. Leach writes: "The snappy American term 'quality time' tells parents they can pack all the desirable interaction with their

For parents who work outside the home, providing quality time may be more myth than reality.

children into a single hour of each working day provided it is a good hour. . . . Of course an hour is better than no time at all and if time is scarce of course it is better not to waste it on chores. But still, the concept of 'quality' time is absurd."7 (See Chapter 6 regarding creating "Special time" with your child.) What most children need and what they thrive upon is the physical presence of a parent during a reasonable portion of their waking lives, which may *include* those precious moments of "quality time."

Your Child as an "Investment"

Few of us ever think of our young children as an investment that will pay future dividends. We save the term for more commercial ventures; we are invested in our jobs, our careers; we make an investment in our homes, or in the stock market. Only when our children reach college age do we think of the cost of their tuition as an investment, and then only as it represents their potential earning power.

But there are far more important returns from an investment in positive, continuing caregiving. We reap the pleasure of being there when our child first speaks, first walks, climbs up the slide, uses the potty, or flops into our arms for comfort and warmth. We are there to touch base to relive our own childhood or try to repair or compensate for what we never experienced. If we manage this investment wisely it can provide wonderful dividends of pleasure and satisfaction at seeing our child, adolescent, and adult thrive. If we do not create a secure foundation for our child, in the end it can become very costly both financially and emotionally.

I do realize that positive parenting requires a considerable "investment" in time and effort. But by making that investment in these crucial early years, not only will a strong bond and secure attachment be forged; the investment will

The first three years of a child's life are crucial to the child's ability to learn.

also lay a firm foundation for the child's later success in school. As the Carnegie Report observes: "We have learned that the fundamental building blocks of school learning must be in place long before" age three.[8] And, the Report points out, "Parents and experts have long known that the first three years of a child's life are crucial to a child's . . . ability to learn."[9]

The investment further pays off as your child becomes an adult who is both loving and responsive to their own future children and spouse. The quality of caregiving is learned primarily from the behavior of the primary attachment figure. In other words, we learn how to be parents from the actions of our own parents. As a result, the early investment in continuity of positive parenting can pay off years later as the child becomes a parent to his or her own child—and your grandchild! Thus, there is a continual and ongoing intergenerational benefit, not only to the families involved but to society as a whole.

George's mother Meg recalls that her parents had a daily ritual of story telling and poetry reading. Meg also created a special time for reading the literature she had learned to love to her son George. Now, George finds that he enjoys the time with his own children to personally reread and recite the poems and literature so important in his childhood. For this family, such intellectual nurturing was passed on for four generations. This love of the written word will probably continue to benefit and enrich their lives for years to come.

The conclusion seems self-evident. Parents for whom the economics of the family make it feasible can say: "For two or three years this is my most important career. If I do my job as primary caregiver well, I will probably have an optimistic and secure child with the ability to learn and to function. And, after a few years, when my child is old enough to understand separations, I will be able to go back to work.

The gift of love: A continuous parental presence during the infant and toddler years.

"But whatever I decide to do in the future, it will be done knowing I have fulfilled my responsibility as a parent by creating the important emotional and cognitive foundation for my child.

I will have given my child the gift of love—my continuous presence during those infant and toddler years, as well as 'being there' in the hours when needed in the years to come."

WHAT TIMMY NEEDS FROM A MOM

I f "Timmy" could tell us what he wants from a parent, he might say:

"I need a mom* with arms that hold me firmly and gently to her heart, a heart that beats along with the familiar waves of her breath.

I need to be rocked, soothed, and sung to, because that dissolves my tension and pain.

I need to fill my emptiness with warmth as I suck to a rhythmic beat.

I need to be allowed to touch, mouth, bang, and toss objects in my world. I need to squeeze, mash, smear, and splash.

I need to trust my world—to know that my mom does not disappear into nothingness, that she is there when I want her.

I need a mom to be there when I wake up angry, sad, or scared, who respects the strength of my cries and is not mad or afraid of me when I am lost in feeling.

I need a mom who, because she is there, senses my aches and fears even before I know them myself—who knows my worries even when I can't tell her.

I need a mom who protects me from danger, is not afraid to say "no," but encourages me to venture forth when it is safe.

I need a mom who allows me to stay close to her. Then I can feel free to toddle off, to risk an adventure, an exploration, or to ponder a new idea.

---

*"Mom" can refer to any caregiver who is committed to raising a child from birth to adulthood.

I need a mom who does not get upset at the mess when I feed myself, yet spoons me my food when I am tired and hungry.

I need a mom who knows when I am ready to say "good-bye" to my diapers, my bottle, or my blanket, who respects my struggle to change, yet encourages my ability to learn new ways.

I need a mom who loves me not only as a baby but as I grow and begin to wail "no" back to her— a mom who is there as I get older, to prepare me for the difficult or strange, to make sense out of what is frightening or painful.

I need a mom to help me learn how to live by the rules, to be loving and caring, a mom I can admire, get mad at, and who will laugh and play.

I need a mom who enjoys my words, expressions, and ideas—who listens with a patient ear even when she can't quite understand.

I need a mom whose anger does not scare or overwhelm me, who shows me the way with firmness and concern yet refrains from hurting my body or soul.

I need a mom who will help me help myself— not use me to allow her to feel powerful—who shows me "how" but is pleased if I can do it my own way.

I need a mom who permits me to be a child, who does not expect me to act as a parent or to be too responsible before I am ready.

But most of all I need a mom who protects, nurtures, and stimulates, who is there with a smile, a hug, and who knows when to leave me alone.

She is a mom that creates a world filled with trust, wonder, and affection—where love flows freely because she is there with me.

Bonding and Attachment:
The Key to Understanding Parent-Infant Behavior

Nature has ingeniously programmed us to respond instinctively to a newborn's immediate need for care and protection. Even the babies of other species— puppies, kittens, fledgling birds, and lion cubs, for example— are adorable and engaging, thereby evoking feelings that arouse the protective response. But human babies need to form a far deeper and longer-lasting bond or attachment with their parents, both for survival and to build the emotional base they need to achieve their potential.

How do infants and parents begin to form this bond? It starts, as psychiatrist John Bowlby's attachment theory postulates, with the earliest and most basic interactions between them. The new parents learn what makes their baby relaxed and contented, or fussy and upset. They learn what actions cause the child to be frightened, what causes pain, what evokes distress. They also become aware of what behavior brings forth smiles, coos, and contentment.

> *Forming an attachment or bond is the main task of the parent or other primary caregiver.*

This process—forging an attachment—is the main task of the parent or other primary caregiver. And it depends for its success (or failure) on hundreds of daily interactions between the infant and his or her primary caregiver.

As we will see, the development of such an attachment is a very personal process that will not occur unless these interactions are confined to the infant and *one* person. And, of course, these many daily, even hourly, interactions are needed to sustain the life of this new human being. But, and this is a big "but," if such interactions occur

Attachment is very personal; to achieve it, hundreds of interactions must occur between the infant and the adult caregiver.

between the infant and five or six persons during an eight- to 10-hour day (as described in Chapter 7), it will be far more difficult (or even impossible) for the infant to form the necessary attachment, no matter how loving and nurturing the care-giver. Of course, an infant may "attach" to more than one per-son—for example, caregiver, mother, and father. But the building of each attachment requires a one-to-one relation-ship over an extended period of time. It is important to keep these concepts in mind as we explore the world of our infant.

The infant must be fed, cleaned, soothed, and stimulated in order to make a successful transition from the protected environment of the womb into an environment where pro-tection and the satisfaction of its needs rests completely on the adults in its new world. Gradually, the newborn begins to expect certain sounds, smells, and movements as the infant anticipates the satisfaction of sucking, nursing, and being held. In close proximity to its protector, the infant associates the repetition of these familiar sounds, smells, and move-ments with his or her physical and emotional satisfaction, and with the reduction of discomfort, pain, and fear.

When a newborn cries, with tiny fists clenched and eyes squeezed shut, it is a signal of distress. The familiar caregiver who provides encompassing arms, a breast, a bottle, or a change of position and who utters comforting sounds or rhythmically walks or rocks the child, provides soothing com-fort that will dispel the distress. And as the caregiver responds to the infant's signals an attachment or bond begins to form. In the mind of the infant it is the beginning of trust. Such "basic trust" (according to the Carnegie Report) "is necessary for healthy psychological development throughout life."[1]

For example, the newborn learns to recognize the smell of the parents (assuming they are the primary caregivers), the sound of their voices, the degree of tension in their arms, and the particular positions in which he or she is held, comforted, and fed. The infant becomes familiar with the way he or she is picked up, jostled, and carried.

Basic trust by an infant is necessary for healthy psychological development throughout life.

It begins to recognize the sounds made by the parent or caregiver—how they breathe, talk, sing, and laugh.

The infant also becomes accustomed to the way its body is cared for: how it is cleaned, diapered, medicated, bathed, and fed. The newborn learns to recognize and anticipate the "response time" of the caregiver. For example, when the infant cries and is quickly picked up, cuddled, and soothed, the infant is able to relax sooner. The proximity of the caregiver to the infant signals protection. The infant feels recognized and acknowledged. He or she is forming the rudiments of a positive self-image, and beginning to trust that its needs will be met.

An infant's first communication is a cry. To emphasize its importance, Bowlby stated that, "when he cries, the mother is likely to take action. For a mother to remain in proximity to an infant and to gather him to her in conditions of alarm clearly serves a protective function."[2] When the baby cries its caregiver becomes aware that the infant is either lonely, hungry, thirsty, wet, ill, or otherwise in some distress, and responds by focusing on and attending to the infant's needs. Commenting upon babies who "seldom cry," Magid and McKelvey state that such an infant, though seeming to be the "perfect baby," may actually be headed for trouble. Because they need less attention, they can set up a cycle that does not promote attachment. A lack of early crying and babbling may result in speech problems later, a common unattached child symptom. A mother or father picking up a crying baby lets him or her know that he or she has power in his or her universe and can do something to relieve stress. This allows the baby to feel he or she is not helpless and alone.[3]

As every parent knows, not all cries are alike. Cries can differ in intensity, quality, pitch, and other subtle variations that parents (or other primary caregivers) learn to recognize. Much has been written about how parents, particularly mothers, become uniquely responsive to their babies, how they learn to differentiate among the wails, squeals, whimpers, and other sounds and to interpret what the babies' cries mean. As a result, these babies in time develop the sense that their world is essentially satisfying, that the people around them are responsive and caring. This positive feeling is the foundation of optimistic attitudes: the feeling that the cup is "half full" rather than "half empty" arises from these early experiences.

Thus in the months following birth, the baby who receives such responsive care gradually develops the ability to trust— the kind of trust that Penelope Leach cites as "the basis of confidence in other people and in self from infancy to death."[4] Gradually the infant learns to wait, even to delay satisfaction and gratification. By three or four months of age, providing he or she has been responded to promptly, a baby may be able to wake without crying and to play with toys, cooing and gurgling, before voicing its first summoning protest or cry.

The Infant's Smile

Just as the baby's cry is a signal of distress that brings the mother to the infant, the baby's smile is a signal that also assures the child of the mother's proximity.

Smiling is essential to a baby's survival.

As every parent knows, these first smiles, which occur at about two months of age, are tremendously satisfying. The smile of the baby is both adorable and compelling; it enlivens and energizes the stressed-out parents. More important, the smile encourages caregiving by triggering impulses in the parents to pick up, hold, fondle, and hug the baby. In this way the baby receives the tactile and kinesthetic stimulation that is not only important physiologically, but that also strengthens the parent-child bond.

Smiling is essential to a baby's survival; a nonresponsive and nonsmiling baby runs the risk of being neglected or ignored. Adults mirror the smile and are stimulated to respond, basking in the glow of their infant's pleasure because they realize that the baby's smile is in response to their presence. As one mother said: "I feel an exquisite, joyful rush of delight when my baby smiles at me."

Confirming this remark, Magid and McKelvey say that "an infant who smiles will start a chain reaction in others, making the whole world smile with him. Smiles and laughter make for a positive environment and set the tone for a future ability to give and receive joy. Early behavior by the infant can have profound effects on how a mother responds. 'But it is the smile that rewards the parent, the smile that decisively seals the emerging bond.'"[5]

Smiling is joined in the third or fourth month by delightful cooing and babbling sounds. These are the beginning of the baby's language development and social responses. In turn, the parents' pleasure in this is manifested by their own sounds and smiles, which provide positive feedback to the infant. This kind of echoing baby talk facilitates a social give and take, which strengthens the attachment process.

Now while it may seem that this interactive process we have outlined is replete with pleasure, it is also true that caring for an infant is often exhausting, sometimes frustrating, and potentially anxiety producing, especially for a first-time parent. But while almost any conscientious substitute caregiver can effectively care for the infant's basic needs, and respond to the positive smiles and sounds, it is the *parent* who is usually going to be better motivated to be responsive to the negative as well as the positive aspects of infant care. It is the *parent*, then, who is far more likely to strengthen the bonding process. This is not meant to denigrate the efforts of the scores of thousands of nonparent caregivers, many if not most of whom perform their duties not only satisfactorily but with concern and, yes, affection for the infant. But even assuming that a substitute caregiver performs well and stays on the job, it is usually the parent who is better motivated to fulfill the task of nurturing and developing a close attachment with his or her infant.

As healthy bonds are forming between parent and infant, a baby—call him Michael—might say (if he could talk):

I feel safe and protected. I feel content because my mommy is near to comfort me. If I am unhappy all I need to do is cry. She will come and do something to make me feel better. Best of all, I feel good when she holds me in her arms and sings to me. I coo back to her and she loves it when I smile and she hears my sounds. I am growing to love her, and I feel lovable as well.

Internal Working Models

Michael sees his world far differently than our baby Timmy saw his. In Bowlby's terms, each child was creating a specific *internal working model* of his world.[6] This means that every child begins to forecast in his own mind how he will be treated in the new world outside the womb. This forecast or expectation is based upon his early interaction experiences with his caregivers. Michael is forming an internal representation in which he feels protected; a positive model of a world in which his caregiver mother is readily accessible and promptly responsive to his needs.

The infant who learns, through experience, to trust, slowly builds, in his or her own mind, a positive internal working model.

He is confident she will attend to him without delay. He is growing to feel not only confident of his parents' affection, but confident also that everyone else finds him lovable. He feels and expects that "his" world is a safe, comfortable, and friendly place, ready and willing to offer him pleasure, protection, and support. In his mind, Michael feels a sense of optimism. His cup is "half full." He has learned, through personal experience, that all will go well for him. He can be confident, courageous, and joyful.

Timmy, on the other hand, constructed an internal working model that forecast little in the way of continuity and predictability of care. Just as Timmy was growing accustomed to his mother and was beginning to bond to her, Betty came along; then Agatha; and then the various ladies at day care. To Timmy, these changes represented three important negative concepts, which he internalized:

- "I can't trust my caregivers. They may not be there when I need them."
- "I feel unprotected and unwanted. I guess I am just unlovable. My world is unpredictable, people come and go and provide little support."
- "I will need to become self-sufficient and not depend on anyone to take care of me."

Because of these negative feelings, Timmy experiences an overwhelming sense of pessimism.

The forecasts that a child makes—his or her working models—depend primarily upon the child's experience with the way caregivers have behaved in the past, and may still be behaving in the present. Bowlby feels that the early attitudes and representations arising from these first relationships are carried forward and influence later (adult) experience. These representations color the child's perceptions and interpretations of events, as well as influence experiences the child seeks out, or tries to avoid. In his book, *Separation*, Bowlby says:

> Thus, an individual who has been fortunate in having grown up in an ordinary good home with ordinarily affectionate parents has always known people from whom he can seek support, comfort, and protection, and where they are to be found. So deeply established are his expectations and so repeatedly have they been confirmed that, as an adult, he finds it difficult to imagine any other kind of world. This gives him an almost unconscious assurance that whenever and

wherever he might be in difficulty, there are always trustworthy figures available who will come to his aid. He will therefore approach the world with confidence, and when faced with potentially alarming situations is likely to tackle them effectively or to seek help in doing so.[7]

But we are particularly concerned here about infants who are confronted with multiple changing caregivers—a situation that undermines their ability to form a secure attachment. These children may create internal working models that forecast a world that is unreliable, untrustworthy, and unpredictable. As a result, they will feel less important, of less value, and less loved by those who have been their caregivers.

Infants and toddlers who learn they cannot trust may feel that all adults are replaceable, love is uncertain, and that human attachment is a dangerous investment.

Unfortunately, this is not simply a childhood perception or attitude. On the contrary, mental health experts tell us that these feelings of unworthiness and pessimism can be a negative force throughout life (see Chapter 4). The unhappy prognosis was eloquently expressed by child expert Selma Fraiberg: In the early years when an infant and his or her parents engage in their first relationships, millions of small children may be learning that all adults are "replaceable, love is uncertain, that human attachment is a dangerous investment."[8]

Stranger Anxiety

At about four to eight months of age, as stronger attachments are forming between infant and parents, or infant and substitute primary caregiver, the child begins to be more selective about those to whom it responds. The baby may actually become agitated and alarmed at the sudden appearance of what seems to the child to be a "stranger." The stranger may be an unfamiliar grandparent or other relative, or an unfamiliar bearded face, or someone who is wearing a new kind of eyeglass frame, or a person with a different skin color; any of these may provoke intense crying and distress.

Some parents are highly upset by this "stranger anxiety" reaction. They worry that their once-sociable child is losing his or her amiability. But this sudden onset of crying and fearful clinging behavior, this turning away from a newcomer, is actually a sign that the baby can now distinguish between the familiar and the unfamiliar. It is a sign of the infant's growing ability to discriminate, and it confirms that the attachment process between baby and parent (or baby and caregiver) is moving along appropriately and normally.

There is, incidentally, a great deal of variation about the time at which stranger anxiety appears. Some babies may happily move from one set of hands to another even as late as the end of the first year; other babies show distress at leaving the familiar for the unfamiliar as early as three months of age.

Stranger anxiety also has survival value. In nature, each species has the capacity to distinguish between what is known as familiar, and therefore safe, from what is different, unknown, and therefore perhaps dangerous. That is why when baby animals are confronted by a different species they quickly run back to their mother for protection and comfort.

Like baby animals, human babies also seek the protection of a parent or familiar caregiver when a "stranger" appears. If the mother projects a warm and affectionate response to the newcomer, thus signaling to the infant that he or she will be safe, the child will more quickly recapture its sense of security. (It also helps to minimize the child's discomfort if newcomers do not "swoop down" and try to hug, hold, or kiss the infant when first arriving on the scene.)

Although the intensity of the "stranger anxiety" reaction diminishes after several months, the attachment and bonding process between infant and parent or caregiver continues to develop and become stronger as the infant grows older. However, stranger anxiety never disappears entirely; it comes and goes throughout the life span. It varies in intensity, depending on the extent of "strangeness" or danger in a particular situation, as well as on the relative degree of secure attachment the individual has developed during his or her *early* life.

The "Secure Base"

Toward the end of the first year, as the bonding process develops and attachment to the caregiver becomes more secure, infants and toddlers will often wander away from the parent to explore their nearby surroundings. This kind of exploration occurs when the infant feels safe and knows where the parent is; the parental presence provides what Mary Ainsworth has described as a "secure base."[9] After an interval of exploration, the baby returns to its parent or caregiver, "checking in," as it were, or "touching base." When the infant feels "restored" by the presence of the adult, he or she will take off once again. This back and forth process continues, with the caregiver providing the emotional anchor so essential for the exploration process.

As the infant becomes attached to the responsive caregiver, confidence and a secure emotional base are established.

Two systems are at work here: one of attachment, and the reciprocal system of exploration. The infant's curiosity pulls him temporarily away from his or her secure base to venture into and experience the outside world. In his book, *Diary Of A Baby*, Daniel Stern dramatically described the feelings of Joey, age one, who wandered off from his mother. Joey says:

And suddenly I am lost. I can't find mommy's stars, and her lines of force have grown weak. The space grows bigger and bigger. It becomes boundless; nothing holds me; I am dissolving like grains of salt in the ocean of space. I panic.

Hearing Joey's summoning call, the mother reunites with him. Joey reports:

> **B**ack with her again, at the sure point, my panic subsides along the skin of my chest and neck. The quieting starts at the surface and flows inward. In the wake of the quieting, I find myself again. The pull of her presence gathers me up out of space. . . . I feel a calming sink in. But slowly I become aware anew of the huge spaces surrounding. Faintly, I hear them call me forth again.[10]

Even as adults, we recognize that having a secure relationship to count on frees us to be more adventuresome, creative, and active. For example, my neighbor's husband was sent on a dangerous wartime mission for the U.S. Navy. During the ten days he was away she found it difficult to leave the house, to read, and even to plan her daily activities. When he returned home she felt as if a gray blanket of anxiety was lifted. Once again she was able to resume her normal expansive existence.

Bowlby asserts that both parents can provide "a secure base from which a child or adolescent can make sorties into the outside world and to which he can return knowing for sure that he will be welcome when he gets there, nourished physically and emotionally, comforted if distressed, reassured if frightened."[11] He also states that "no parent is going to be able to provide a 'secure base' for the child unless he has an intuitive understanding and respect for the child's attachment behavior and treats it as an intrinsic and valuable part of human nature."[12]

A secure attachment is reinforced when a parent who has left the child in a strange environment returns and picks up the child, trying to soothe and caress and accept the child's sadness and anger. However, if the parent rebuffs and ridicules the child instead of giving comfort when he or she shows distress, that parent is not displaying understanding or respect for the child's feelings of anxiety. By failing to comfort the child, such a parent undermines the formation of a secure base, and effectively curtails the child's exploratory behavior.

In later chapters, we will show how creating a secure base by providing a child with the continuous positive presence of a mother or primary caregiver frees the child not only to explore his or her physical environment, but also to be playful, absorbed, curious, and open to all kinds of learning and mastery of experiences.

Discussing the creation of a secure base and its relationship to a *few* dependable adults, the Carnegie Report states: "During the first three years of life, much has to be acquired, much mastered, much tried and found wanting, much discovered and put to use. Ideally, this learning time is spent in close relationship with adults who offer nurturing love, protection, guidance, stimulation and support. For the caregivers it is an enduring long-term highly challenged commitment. Rearing by a few caring, responsive, dependable adults leads to strong attachments and provides a secure base from which the infant can explore the larger, social and physical world. Such secure early attachments are essential for human development."[13]

> **Parents who have provided a secure base for their infant help them to successfully explore and function in their larger social and physical world.**

Separation Anxiety

Separation anxiety occurs when the infant suddenly feels unprotected and the attachment figure or parent is unavailable for comfort. As we have seen, when infants or toddlers feel secure they are more likely to explore their surroundings and move away from the caregiver; when they are tired, anxious, alarmed, or unwell they feel an urge to be close to parent or caregiver. But what happens when the caregiver leaves the toddler? This is a different matter altogether.

If the parent or caregiver moves to a different room, or shuts a door that is between the child and the grown-up, a storm of crying and protest may erupt. This reaction is called "separation anxiety." It can occur when, from the child's point of view, the parent is inaccessible, not available for comfort and protection. The crying, screaming, clutching, clinging, or other active attempts to find the parent or get the caregiver's attention may be intense. Typically, a mother may not even be able to close the bathroom door for a moment for her own privacy without causing cries of distress and outrage from her toddler.

This protest is the child's declaration of the mother's special value to him or her. We tend to think of these protests negatively (as we sometimes do that of stranger anxiety) because the child's emotional reaction is so strong and demanding. But, in fact, anger at separation can be considered a positive response because it validates the bond between parent (or caregiver) and child, and indicates that it has been developing appropriately. When the parent reappears the protest usually stops; the child once again feels comforted by the parent's presence. Such a strong protest reaction to separation is normal, and is to be expected from children from about one to three years of age.

If a child in the second year of life fails to show any such signs of distress, or fails to act wary when the parent or primary caregiver takes leave, it may be an indication that the child has *not* formed a close relationship with that person. It may also mean that the child has become "detached" or "avoidant" and that he or she did not develop a secure attachment and bond to a primary caregiver in the critical first years.

In the child's first year of life, all parents must separate from the infant for varying periods of time and for varying reasons: to make a phone call, go to the market, to a movie, to a meeting, to work, recreating, or traveling. And even though infants and toddlers may loudly "protest," they *can* tolerate short intervals of separation. After all, parents and caregivers need to have some respite from the hour-to-hour and day-to-day commitment to their infants. However, long periods of time away from the child—working, recreating, traveling—can cause a more profound reaction, one that heightens the degree of separation anxiety.

One thing parents can do to minimize the pain of separation anxiety is to prepare their child, especially during the second six months of life, to tolerate absences and separations. One example is by verbalizing a "good-bye" routine. The parent may, before leaving, say "Bye-bye, I'm going to the store now" (or to the bank, or post office); or, "Bye-bye, I'm going to the kitchen" (or bathroom, or upstairs).

Providing a "good-bye" routine can help minimize the pain of separation.

The child may not understand the actual words, but the sounds begin to mean that a separation will occur.

Although it may seem easier to "sneak out" and avoid the noisy protest, such conduct can erode the child's trust. When the child discovers the parent has left *without* the "good-bye" or similar routine, the child feels he or she cannot rely upon the parents' presence. The child may now feel it is necessary to keep a constant vigil, with one eye always on the parent or caregiver.

But if the parent faithfully prepares the child with the expected "good-bye" routine, the child can more easily feel safe, relaxed, and trusting. He or she now knows the parent will not suddenly disappear *without the routine warning*. Preparing a child for brief separations in this way not only shows respect for the child's feelings, but also helps prevent the child from becoming "anxiously attached," a condition we will explain in a moment.

Separation anxiety is not confined to the first few years. This emotional response may come and go throughout the life span. Like stranger anxiety, it also varies in intensity and depends upon the extent of strangeness and degree of danger perceived in a particular situation. It also depends on the relative security of other attachments the child has developed during its early life. Starting preschool, going to kindergarten or a summer camp program, or being left at a birthday party or sleepover can reactivate this strong anxiety. Even adolescents who leave on a trip, or who are expected to sally forth independently on an adventure or enter a new school or college, can suffer the same pain of separation. Nor are adults exempt from experiencing this strong emotion when feeling alone and unprotected.

Separation anxiety can occur at any age.

During natural disasters many persons are affected more intensely if they are alone and separated from loved ones. Indeed, separation anxiety can strike at any age and under any circumstance when we feel unprotected and separated from our attachment figure.

Patterns of Attachment: Secure, Anxious, and Detached

Many psychologists have attempted to classify patterns of attachment. The first research that describes such patterns was pioneered by child psychologist Dr. Mary Ainsworth in the early 1960's. She structured a laboratory procedure known as "the Strange Situation," where she could observe both the child's response to separation and the child's response to reuniting with the attachment figure.[14] Ainsworth identified three patterns: secure attachment, anxious resistant attachment, and anxious avoidant attachment. It must be noted that the research was done with mother-child pairs and not with substitute caregivers. Other psychologists, such as Mary Main, Alan Sroufe, and Alicia Lieberman, have also tried to describe various patterns of attachment.

But, regardless of the psychological classifications used by these authorities, I feel it may be more useful to think of attachment as part of a continuum with secure attachment at one end and the detached child at the other extreme. An important objective of positive parenting is to try to provide the most secure attachment for the child.

Before describing the various patterns of attachment, it should be understood that each child is endowed with a unique temperament and sensitivity to stimuli. Children are born with individual personalities that respond to separation with differing intensities. Each child's perceived need for protection in new or frightening situations varies. It is also true that temperamental differences in each child can create difficulties in the bonding process. Babies may be fussy if they are allowed to cry longer or are handled more roughly than placid infants, resulting in a less secure attachment. On the other hand, quiet babies may be ignored or not be sufficiently stimulated to create a close bond.

Also, the time it takes for each child to feel secure may differ in unfamiliar environments. However, the responsive parent or caregiver learns to know and respect these individual characteristics as they attempt to create a secure base for their child.

Furthermore, at times almost every child may show the specific behaviors of the anxious, avoidant, or detached child. The unusual and disturbing behavior parents observe may be due to a combination of their child's unique temperament and sensitivities as well as the environmental stresses and pressures they experience at the time, or in the immediate past.

The patterns of attachment we are about to discuss were observed in children in their second year. These patterns seemed to persevere and be relatively consistent throughout life. It is felt by most attachment theorists that the quality of the child-caregiver relationship is a primary factor in determining the patterns of attachment behavior, and that it remains relatively constant during the child's growing years.

The child with a secure attachment feels able to explore a strange environment. This ability can carry over into adult life.

The child with a secure attachment is able to explore a strange environment, may protest when separation occurs, but when the mother or caregiver returns, her comforting presence enables the child to go back to exploration or interactive play. When minor stress is introduced, these children are not unduly wary. But, after separation from the mother they quickly and effectively seek her out and are reassured by her presence. As previously stated, secure attachment is promoted by a parent who is attuned to the child's signals and is responsive when the child needs comfort and protection. Thus it follows that the unpredictable comings and goings of a parent and the introduction of different caregivers is detrimental to the formation of such a secure attachment.

Julia, 22 months old, was a child with a secure attachment. On a visit to a new home, she stayed close to her mom. Julia needed to sit on her mother's lap for about five minutes in order to feel comfortable. The unfamiliar adult brought out some toys and placed them on the floor. Soon Julia squirmed off her mom and began to manipulate the objects. Every so often she would look at her mom and return her interests to the toys. After a short time elapsed, Julia was asked if she wanted some apple juice. She accompanied the host into the kitchen and returned to her mother holding her cup. Suddenly, the door opened and the husband of the friend returned with their large dog. Julia was frightened and immediately retreated to her mother. She started to cry. Her mother quickly picked her up, comforted her, held her close and cheerfully exclaimed: "What a beautiful doggie you have." After a while Julia stopped crying, feeling protected in her mother's arms, and soon became fascinated with the fluffy dog moving about. Subsequently, at another visit to the same house, Julia was able to pat the dog and not experience the original panic.

An anxiously attached child is uncertain whether the parent will be available or responsive when called upon. Such anxiously attached infants are less able to use the caregiver as a secure base for exploration because they feel their attachment figure is inaccessible or unresponsive. Usually the more stable or predictable the care, the more secure a child's attachment tends to be; but the more discontinuous, unreliable, and unpredictable the care, the more anxious is the attachment to the primary caregiver.

C onsider 14-month-old Jennifer, who never leaves her mother's side when they go to the park. Even though her mother encourages her, she is afraid to move from the bench where her mother sits and go to the nearby sandbox to play. She is so unwilling to lose physical contact that she literally stays touching her mother's body. Jennifer does not feel secure even when her mother is present; she remains constantly vigilant to the threat of separation. Exploratory behavior does not occur. Nor are the pleasures of the park available to Jennifer because of her abiding need to cling to her mother.

Children like Jennifer who were identified as anxious in the strange situation experiment were reluctant to separate from the mother despite an array of attractive toys. They were upset when the mother left them, and could not be comforted by her when she returned. They continued to fuss, and even when they were picked up and held they squirmed away in anger. They never were able to regain their emotional balance sufficiently well so that they could go back to play.

Basically, they are in a constant state of anxiety, uncertain whether their parents will be there to offer support when needed. Clinging and unwillingness to venture forth characterizes the behavior of the anxious child. This behavior can occur when a parent is sometimes available and responsive but at other times is rejecting, unhelpful, and unsupportive. For example, when leaving for school in the morning, these children have difficulty in saying good-bye to their parents. They do not easily become connected either to other children or to play activities at school. Unfortunately, they may be pre-occupied by thinking about when their mom or dad will pick them up. They do not benefit nearly as much from their school experience as the "secure" child who feels free to concentrate and to relate to classmates and teachers.

In contrast, avoidant or detached children expect to be rejected and rebuffed by their caregivers. They try to become emotionally self-sufficient and self-reliant. Timmy, in Chapter 1, at 18 months, is a good example of this pattern of attachment. Children like Timmy are often described as "detached." They easily separate from their mothers and can begin playing with toys. They are usually not wary when a stranger appears. Nor do they cry when mother leaves the scene. However, when the mother does return, these children actively avoid her. They increase their distance from her, and continue to reject contact with her. The greater the stress, the more they avoid letting her comfort them. Sroufe and Waters found (by measuring heart rate) that such detached infants remained upset when the caregiver returned. This was in contrast to the secure group who were quickly comforted and restored by their mothers' presence.[15]

....

Some detached children are like Barbara, age two, who had a chaotic attachment history with multiple caregivers by the time she was 16 months old. It was difficult to get her attention. She never looked at you but seemed obsessed with what she wanted. When frustrated over not getting something that she needed, she would scream yet could not be comforted or soothed, even when she finally got her way. Barbara did not respect normal boundaries but even at an early age repeatedly climbed out of her crib. Often, as a toddler, she ran out of the house and put herself in dangerous predicaments. Her mother reported that she soothed herself by banging her head rhythmically. Not only was she detached, but her behavior was aggressive and rejecting to her adult caregivers. No one liked her, and yet she was only two. She was often referred to as "the bad seed," "Miss Trouble," or "a devil." It is not unusual for children like Barbara to grow up without the ability to give or receive affection, showing cruelty to others and engaging in self-destructive behavior. It is easy to see what a dismal future lies ahead for Barbara. Even with intense therapeutic intervention, the prognosis is grim.

For a child like Barbara, avoiding frequent changes of environments and caregivers would have helped to provide a more secure attachment. By contrast, unpredictable nonresponsive care, frequent changes of caregivers, multiple losses, and long-term separations predisposed her to develop an extreme degree of detachment, avoidant and negative behavior.

Bowlby points out that a pattern "once developed, tends to persist," and that each such pattern tends to be self-perpetuating because "the way a parent treats a child tends to continue unchanged." Clearly then, the environment created by parents—rather than heredity—is the more important factor and it persists with long-term ramifications. Bowlby states "that stability of pattern, when it occurs, cannot be attributed to the child's inborn temperament as has been sometimes claimed. Nevertheless, as a child grows older, the pattern becomes the property of the child himself which means that he tends to impose it, or some derivative of it, upon new relationships such as a teacher, foster mother or therapist."[16]

Bowlby therefore feels that a child internalizes such a pattern and thus produces predictable consistency in attachment behavior.

The Legacy of Separations and Losses: Protest, Despair, and Detachment

We are all familiar with the strong emotions evoked when a parent leaves a child in the hands of another person. The child's immediate reaction to this separation from the parent or attachment figure is usually to "protest" by crying, scream-ing, and acting enraged. This behav-ior is intense, noisy, and intrusive. Its purpose is to summon the parent or caregiver back, to restore their

Protest behavior can be intense and noisy.

close proximity to the child. But after a few days of intermit-tent protestations and outbursts, when the parent does not reappear, the child seems to give up the explosive behavior, and lapse into sadness, depression, and despair. These reac-tions are primarily a result of the infant's or toddler's anxiety and concern when the child does not feel the presence, com-fort, and support of the familiar parent.

The lack of language, the level of comprehension, and the inability to communicate further intensifies the separation for the young child. Without the ability to understand, young children begin to feel the parent will never return. Remember, after Timmy's first baby-sitter left him, he reacted by sleeping much of the time. He did not crawl around and explore as he did before she suddenly left. He was depressed and despairing. Films made in England in the 1950s by James Robertson (a social worker interested in studying sep-aration) illustrate the impact of separations upon "normal" 18-month-old children. The films dramatically depict how these children, day by day, became sad, withdrawn, and immobilized while their mother stayed in the hospital for ten days.[17] Of the child aged from eighteen to twenty-four months Robertson writes:

If a child is taken from his mother's care at this age, when he is so possessively and passionately attached to her, it is indeed as if his world had been shattered. His intense need of her is unsatisfied, and the frustration and longing may send him frantic with grief. It takes an exercise of imagination to sense the intensity of this distress. He is as overwhelmed as any adult who has lost a beloved person by death. To the child of two with his lack of understanding and complete inability to tolerate frustration it is really as if the mother had died. He does not know death, but only absence; and if the only person who can satisfy his imperative need is absent, she might as well be dead, so overwhelming is his sense of loss.[18]

In responding to a child's loss, substitute caregivers may be relieved when the intense protest reactions stop and the inac-

When crying stops, the child may still be in pain.

tivity or depression takes over. The young child becomes less difficult to handle, sleeps more, and causes less disruption. However, the young child is still in pain, but is expressing it differently. It is akin to adults mourning a loss; waves of sadness come and go.

After an increased separation of three or four weeks, a child who was initially angry, then sad, may appear cold, aloof, and unresponsive. This child will eventually become what is termed "detached." As a response to the pain of prolonged separation, the child acts emotionally wounded and as protection from the pain, begins to behave as if he or she no longer feels or cares. He or she finds ways to be amused or comforted through solitary play or self-soothing behavior (obsessive thumb sucking, masturbation, rocking, hair twirling, and head banging). This process of detachment has lifelong implications. All through adulthood, such detached children will have problems with trust, thereby preventing close and intimate relationships from developing and being sustained. They feel that they must rely only on themselves, that they must be completely self-sufficient and reject their need for comfort and support (see Chapter 4). At times their simmering rage will unpredictably erupt, causing an increased alienation of those individuals in their immediate environment.

Long-Term Separations

Long-term separations, especially with infants and toddlers, require even more careful consideration and planning. To a child in the second year of life, especially if he or she cannot yet verbalize, a separation longer than a day or so may be stressful. The reason: children at this age have not yet developed a sense of time. Yet, work commitments often require parents to be away overnight, or even for two or three nights. Such separations increase anxiety in preverbal children; they simply cannot understand the meaning of a three-day (or longer) separation. The child experiences this separation as an abandonment, and reacts with a sense of worry, anxiety, and anger.

Consider an analogous situation in a marriage where a spouse leaves for work in the morning and stays away for three days and nights without a word or a phone call. The spouse left at home will probably first feel worried, then feel angry, and eventually conclude that something terrible—an accident or a crime—has occurred. Concern, fear, and pain would grow. But adults have resources to deal with such a situation: they can make a phone call, question friends or relatives, call the police. The toddler, having no resources for coping, simply suffers intensely.

If parents must be away from a toddler for more than a few days, they should not be surprised if the child at first turns away and is tentative with them when they return. Parents can also anticipate that the child will demonstrate a high level of negative behavior—clinging, whining, protesting—in the days following the separation. It helps if parents can plan trips that include the child. Such arrangements will surely pose inconveniences, but the child will benefit from the sustained continuity with the parents. For example:

Pauline and her husband took a three-week pleasure/business trip. They could not easily afford the expense of bringing along a sitter, so they arranged for one in the hotel. Pauline worried less since she was with her child during part of each day and night. Needless to say, the toddler was also more content when reunited with his parents after the brief daily separations than he would have been if separated from his parents for three weeks while they were traveling.

If any separations must occur (for example, death or illness of a family member) during the second year, a familiar caregiver brought into the child's home will help ease the stress. So will creating a scrapbook including pictures of mother or father; pictures of the car, plane, or train; as well as pictures of where the parent is going (hotel room, etc.) These can be shown to the child, along with verbal reassurances that mommy or daddy "is coming back." Preparing a videotape can be helpful. Using a standard camcorder, a parent or caregiver can read or tell a favorite story which can repeatedly be played back for the child. On the tape the parent or caregiver can speak reassuringly about returning home. The tape will help the child to create visual images that will structure the coming separation and reduce the child's distress. Phone calls home (even with resulting protests and crying) can also help lessen anxiety. Even though the child cannot verbalize, he or she can hear the voices and see the picture of the parents. Both help keep the image of the parent alive for the child.

When hired primary caregivers change, an infant or toddler will experience severe emotional stress because these caregivers are usually never seen again. For the infant, the permanent loss of such a substitute caregiver, with whom an attachment was formed, is similar to experiencing the death of a close family member. The infant will experience feelings and display behavior associated with mourning.

When substitute caregivers leave, they may never be seen again.

As we have seen, long-term separations and losses combine to erode a child's sense of trust. The child comes to feel he or she cannot risk a relationship for fear of losing it, and may become anxious, withdrawn, or detached as a defense against the pain of such loss. It is also true that becoming detached or displaying negative behavior can also be a defense against the pain of relating to a parent or caregiver who is present but is abusive, punitive, and/or who does not protect the child. For a toddler to trust and feel close to such a parent is simply too risky.

Our discussion of attachment theory has focused primarily on the infant and toddler. But attachment behavior is in no way confined to young children. In times of stress older children, adolescents, and adults actively seek support, comfort, and protection from caregiver, parent, friend, or spouse. This activation of attachment behavior is universal and normal. Even the most cursory survey of literature, theater, and popular music yields recurrent themes concerning attachment: the pain of rejection, the joy of reunion, the sadness of loss, the fear and anguish of separation, and finally the hope and longing for reciprocal love.

Attachment theory supplies us with an understanding of the abiding need for secure attachments, the profound significance of separation and loss, and the lifelong importance of our relationships with others. Bowlby explains the significance of attachment in this way: "Throughout adult life the availability of a responsive attachment figure remains the source of a person's feeling secure. All of us, from the cradle to the grave, are happiest when life is organized as a series of excursions, long or short, from the secure base provided by our attachment figure(s)."[19]

What Happens When Caregivers Change:
The Dangers of "Caregiver Roulette"

A glance at any newspaper, or a few minutes spent listening to any radio or television news program, quickly confirms the fact—if, indeed, it needs confirming—that this country faces serious social problems, and that many of them directly concern our young people: increasingly poor school performance and increasing dropout rates; crime and violence; juvenile delinquency spreading into middle-class neighborhoods; drug and alcohol addiction; mental illnesses, including but not limited to depression and anxiety; adolescent alienation; and difficulties with personal relationships.

These serious problems were dramatically described by the noted child-care authority Dr. T. Berry Brazelton during a television discussion on the Oprah Winfrey Show on May 16, 1995. Dr. Brazelton said, "Never before has one generation been less healthy, less cared for, less prepared for life than their parents were at the same age."[1]

These sentiments were supported by the Children's Defense Fund in its 1995 *The State of America's Children Yearbook*,[2] which indicated that 7.7 million American children suffer from serious emotional disorders. The *Yearbook* explained that 48 percent of this group, virtually half, will eventually drop out of high school. And sadder still, a full 73 percent of these dropouts will be arrested within five years of leaving school.[3]

But there is little agreement about what causes these social ills. Some blame disintegrating family values and the decline of the two-parent family. Others blame uncaring teachers and a bureaucratic, underfunded school system; others blame films and television for their emphasis on violence. Still others blame poverty and an unstable economy.

Obviously there is no one single or simple answer for these complex problems. But there is one contributing factor—one element in the mix—that is being overlooked. That factor is the discontinuity of care our infants and toddlers receive. I believe that frequent changes of caregivers in a child's first three years of life are an important cause of poor attachment and bonding. The conse-

Caregiver roulette— the frequent change of primary caregivers—can cause life-long and severe emotional damage.

quences of such a failure is one precipitating factor in the development of all the problems mentioned above.

It may be hard for most people to accept the idea that something that happens between birth and the age of three—something as seemingly unimportant as a change in caregivers—can have such an enormous effect on a child's life, both during childhood and in his or her later, adolescent, and even adult years.

But, as we pointed out in Chapters 2 and 3, there is a very good reason why frequent changes of caregivers—which I call "caregiver roulette"—can do significant emotional damage to preverbal children. The reason: when caregivers change it is impossible to prepare the infants or toddlers involved because they have not yet acquired the ability to communicate verbally. Therefore, they cannot be prepared for the departure of a caregiver, whether mother or substitute. When change does occur—which may be experienced as a profound loss by the child—his or her trust in the world is shaken. The child creates an expectation or "internal working model" (discussed in Chapter 3) that it is not safe to trust. In addition, the preverbal child cannot communicate to the parent the quality of the care he or she received during the parent's absence nor the specific experiences that occurred during this most vulnerable period.

In this chapter we will cite experts in child development who have studied and researched this issue. We also find confirmation in the recent Carnegie Report. Speaking of the value of consistent early care, it says that such a "good start in life measurably decreases the risk that individuals will drop out of school . . . or shuttle in and out of the criminal justice system. All of society benefits when young children grow up to be productive, secure, active citizens."[4]

Except for the very wealthy, "dependable" family retainers are a thing of the past. As a result, today's caregivers—baby-sitters, nannies, housekeepers, au pairs, day-care workers, neighbors or relatives who help out—every one who interacts with an infant or toddler, while the parents are at work, changes with mind-numbing frequency. A 1990 University of California study found that even at the "best" day-care centers, the turnover rate for caregivers was very high—over 40 percent annually.[5] Another child care authority, Marcy Whitebook said that "[t]urnover among child care workers is second only to parking lot and gas station attendants."[6] Surely we can offer our children a better quality of care than we give our automobiles!

The Carnegie Report further confirms the dangers to infants and toddlers of frequent changes in caregivers by noting that such "turnover has consequences for infants and toddlers: 'what we call turnover' Deborah Phillips, an expert in child development said, 'they experience as loss.'"[7] The same Carnegie Report, commenting on the small wages paid to child-care givers states: "We pay higher salaries in our society to people to take care of dogs in kennels and cars in parking lots than to the adults who take care of our children in child-care."[8]

People who take care of dogs in kennels earn more than those caring for children.

As we consider "turnover" of caregivers and its consequences, we should keep in mind that turnover, or change, has many forms—some quite subtle and unappreciated. As we will see in the discussion in Chapter 7, on selection of substitute care, the "best" day-care centers can unwittingly compound a caregiver "roulette" process because of their very laudable concerns in providing a low caregiver-to-infant ratio. Such a policy requires more trained personnel: obviously if the infant-to-caregiver ratio is the preferred one-to-three, more such caregivers are needed than if, say, a one-to-seven ratio is provided. But such care is tiring and demanding. To help such staff members, there are breaks, staggered shifts, rotation of personnel, and other measures, which can result in an infant being cared for by six or more persons in one day! And remember, from the infant's standpoint, this variety of change is in addition to all the others already described.

Nor should we forget another basic truth about why infant day care is structured as it is. Dr. Leach says it best: "The truth is that institutional day care offers advantages to adults that have nothing to do with an infant's safety or happiness."[9] Such disregard for the needs of our infants and toddlers means we are increasingly denying them the opportunity to form the secure emotional attachments that are so vital to their lives, both now and in the future.

Other authorities agree: Dr. Edward Zigler, director of the Bush Center for Child Development and Social Policy at Yale University. Zigler, who was a founder of the Head Start program in the United States, suggests that the years children spend in subpar day care is a major cause of the largest rise in the incidence of child violence and depression that experts in mental health have ever seen.[10]

> *The years children spend in subpar day care is a major cause of child violence and depression.*

A most disturbing report on child day-care centers was published in April 1995 by the University of Colorado. This report contained the findings of child-care authorities at four major universities (the University of Colorado, the University of California, the University of North Carolina, and Yale University). The report stated that at most child-care centers "the levels of quality required to support children's development are not being met." Of the 401 centers studied, only "14% were rated as developmentally appropriate—while the remaining 86% scored from poor to mediocre."[11]

The report dramatically describes the problem as a "silent crisis largely unacknowledged by American families or the American public. The crisis stems from our inattention to the quality of child care—an inattention that carries with it profound costs in human and economic terms. The majority of American children who are in child care centers spend many hours in mediocre quality settings that are detrimental to their development . . . [T]he American public, although adoring young children . . . blindly engages in self-deception about child care quality so great it could be deemed societal child neglect."[12] The report concludes that such child care in 1995 may be of even lower quality as compared to that of 1989, when a similar study was carried out.[13]

Child-care authority Professor Burton White of Harvard University put it this way: "After more than 20 years of research on how children develop well, I would not think of putting a child of my own into any substitute care program on a full time basis, especially a center based program."[14]

One must understand that the pros and cons of day care, as well as other substitute care, have been a matter of hot debate among psychologists and other day-care authorities. Both Dr. Jay Belsky, of Pennsylvania State University, and Dr. Zigler, of Yale University, have voiced deep concern about the effects of day care upon young children. Dr. Belsky has even quantified the risks, estimating that the danger point is 20 hours per week or more of such care for children under age one.[15]

More than 20 hours of day care per week can be dangerous.

The adverse consequences of day care reported by Belsky may be accounted for not so much because infants and toddlers were placed in substitute care per se but more because of the lack of "quality" and "stability" of such care. Indeed, such a conclusion was voiced by Dr. Carollee Howes and P. Stewart in a 1986 study of 55 toddler-aged children. They concluded that "stability of childcare arrangements is more important than the age the child begins childcare." They also said that "children who changed childcare arrangements more often were less confident in their play with peers" and that infants "who had few childcare changes were most likely to engage in high level play."[16] Psychologist Alan Sroufe has also commented that "Given the current status of the evidence on timing and the quality of daycare, we would favor more choices being available to parents, so that full time daycare is not the only option for those with young children."[17]

In fact, study after study that I have reviewed reveals that substitute care facilities, whether run-of-the-mill day-care centers or high quality university-based centers, and even nannies in upper-middle-class homes, often seem to share one common problem: caregivers in such settings change very frequently. And it is quite irrelevant to the children involved whether such changes are described as: "lack of stability," "turnover of child-care personnel," or "poor quality day care." It is the unpredictability of the environment that causes the distress for infants and toddlers.

Day care, whether rendered by the most prestigious university centers, or ordinary "nanny-care," often suffers from one important defect: the factor I call caregiver roulette. The infant or toddler never knows in whose arms he or she will land. When these arms change frequently, the children are more likely to experience emotional distress with the concomitant potential for problems later in life. This is especially true if they experience multiple losses of the persons who care for them.

For those children where continuity and predictability of primary substitute care is provided, negative effects are minimized. In such an ideal world of substitute care, the beloved substitute caregiver has a close and nurturing relationship with the infant or toddler. This relationship continues without disruption at least until the child is verbal—which is approximately age two or three. At this point in the child's development, the child can understand that the departure of the caregiver is not an abandonment or "desertion," although the child may still experience the sadness of the loss.

But in the real world of substitute caregiving, such stability, continuity, and consistency is difficult to provide, and is the reason for the failure of most substitute care today.

I realize that to the lay person it may seem unlikely, if not totally farfetched, that caregiver roulette and inconsistent parenting could predispose their child to future problems. Yet many child-care professionals agree that at least five major social ills stem in part from such lack of continuity and from the consequent poor attachment between very young children and their parents and/or caregivers.

We must be aware that these social ills also can occur in families where the mother or father stayed home and did provide continuity of care. Yet these parents may not have been sufficiently attuned to or sensitive to their child's needs. Even with a parent present, a secure attachment may not develop—perhaps because of a lack of responsiveness to the child. However, the probability of such social ills occurring appears to be higher with frequently changing substitute caregivers.

It is also true that every child is uniquely endowed with individual strengths, gifts, weaknesses, and handicaps. Each child is born into a family that varies in the ability to nurture and where fortune plays *its* part in the child's future.

Because of the multitude of variables influencing these problems, the consequences of caregiver roulette cannot be reduced to a statistical certainty. But it must be considered as one important and often overlooked factor in the attachment process.

Let us look in a bit more detail at these major problem areas.

School Problems

We all know, hear about, or read about children who are either aggressive or withdrawn in class, who refuse to do their homework, who are such frequent troublemakers they are sent to the principal's office to be disciplined, and who bring home poor report cards. Such children, we are told, cannot get enough attention from their teacher. Others are "detached," distant children who have difficulty making friends.

Educators at all levels—preschool, elementary, and high school—are concerned about disruptive classroom behavior, falling standardized-test scores, and the growing rate of school dropouts. "Teachers report that 35% of American kindergarten children arrive at school unprepared to learn," according to the Carnegie Report.[18] But the family histories of these children reveal that many of them did not have stability or continuity of care in the years from birth through age three. Nor did they have consistent or appropriate supervision in the succeeding years. Many had multiple caregivers and experienced frequent separations from one or both parents.

> **35% of American kindergarten children arrive unprepared to learn.**

As mentioned previously, Dr. Jay Belsky studied the effects of nonmaternal day care in an infant's first year and voiced concern about infants who spent over 20 hours per week in such care. Since nonmaternal care is statistically associated with lack of caregiving continuity, Belsky's conclusion seems particularly appropriate. He concluded "that entry into care in the first year of life is a risk factor for the development of insecure avoidant attachments in infancy, and heightened aggressiveness, non-compliance and withdrawal in the preschool and early school years."[19]

Another investigator, psychologist Alan Sroufe, noted the poor functioning of anxiously attached children who suffered early bonding defects: "Children who were anxiously attached as infants functioned more poorly in preschool than did children who were securely attached."[20] On the other hand, Sroufe observed that "Children securely attached as infants were found to be more ego resilient, independent, compliant, empathic and socially competent; they had greater self esteem and expressed more positive affect and less negative affect than did children who were anxiously attached as infants."[21] Children described as anxiously attached or detached have great difficulty listening to teachers, establishing eye contact with teachers or classmates, following instructions, and concentrating on schoolwork. Yet these are the very abilities that are essential if children are to progress successfully through our educational system.

John Bowlby summed up the unhappy prognosis in the following way. Commenting upon children who fail to develop secure attachments, Bowlby's assessment is disturbing: education of such children is impossible because of their lack of capacity to form relationships.[22]

Clearly, it is much harder for a child to bond with or even develop positive feelings toward a teacher if, in his or her first years, the child was never able to trust the adults in his or her world. When a child has been deprived of secure emotional relationships as an infant and toddler, or a child experiences a great deal of anger and rage at his or her parents, the ability to trust and bond to teachers (or other authority figures) is undermined. If an infant or toddler has been compelled to experience loss after loss, as caregivers come and go, the child is also being taught that he or she should be wary of any adults (teachers included). Conversely, good feelings toward a mother or other consistent caregiver can transfer to positive feelings toward teachers and other adults and learning can take place.

A history of insecure attachments augurs poorly for later school success as well. As adolescents, with no strong connection to school or teachers, these youngsters tend to drop out of school. Others simply go through the motions until they leave formal education. Saddest of all, as adults without the positive school experiences they might have had, many never function at anything near their education potential. Psychiatrist John L. Weil confirmed the serious effects of early maternal deprivation on academic functioning in the teen years: "The adolescent with a history of chronic deprivation during infancy" may have experiences that trigger responses "of turning away from visual contact and from auditory contact." Such children "often will do poorly in school because of difficulties in paying attention to his or her teacher's lectures."[23] And indeed, how often do we hear teachers and parents complain about such teenagers' behavior:

"They won't look at me." "They never seem to listen." "I can't seem to teach them at all."

The more one reads the research studies, and the more one talks with teachers and parents, the more the evidence mounts until the conclusion is irrefutable: preschool children, infants, and toddlers who have been exposed to inconsistent care suffer a host of learning deficits. They have poor cognitive skills. They may also take longer to learn to talk. They may lack age-appropriate knowledge. For example:

- Professor Carollee Howes at the University of California conducted two studies of 18- to 24-month-old children who had been cared for in their own homes or in family day-care homes. She found that most of them had already lived through two or three changes in caregivers, and some as many as six. Howes found that the more changes the children experienced, the more trouble they had adjusting to first grade.[24]

- As I did research for this book, preschool and elementary school teachers told me that they were finding a lack of maturity in language expression. Some teachers believed the children were often deprived of listening to their mothers talk on the telephone, in the market, to neighbors, and to family members. Many children had caregivers whose primary language was foreign, and, as a result, they received less reinforcement in English language stimulation.

- In conversations I have had with many preschool teachers in middle-class schools, I hear them repeatedly express their distress at the fact that many three- and four-year-olds show a serious gap in their general knowledge. Absentee parents are not as available as in the past to teach their children those concepts characteristic of the preschool child (colors, shapes, opposites, directions, parts of bodies, and so on).

- Many of these same teachers report that when a child first enters school—usually an emotionally difficult time—he or she is often brought by a baby-sitter, not by a parent. Not having a parent present at this important rite of passage may tell the child that his or her school and education is not important enough to merit the attendance of mother or father. This is a subtle devaluing of the child's school experience.

But perhaps the most convincing evidence of the link between caregiver roulette and poor school performance comes from a long-term study conducted by the Frank Porter Graham Child Development Center at the University of North Carolina and reported by R. Haskins.[25] Jay Belsky confirms that this study reinforces all the findings of the negative effects of caregiver changes in the first year of life. The North Carolina researchers studied kindergartners and first graders who had been cared for, starting at age three months, at the "extremely high quality daycare center at the University of North Carolina." The study compared this group with other children who also experienced nonmaternal childcare but not until "some time after the first year of life."[26]

> **There is a link between caregiver roulette and poor school performance.**

The study supplies convincing evidence that early exposure, at age three months, to such "center" based day care (with the inevitable use of multiple changing caregivers), produces results that are long-term and unfortunate: the children showed more aggressive behavior. They were more likely to "hit, kick and push" than other children. They were also more likely to "threaten, swear and argue." Teachers also noted that children in this group were less likely to walk away to "avoid or extract themselves from situations that could lead to aggression." Their teachers were more likely to describe these children as having "a serious deficit in social behavior."[27]

Timmy, our hypothetical youngster in Chapter 1, may prove to be much like those problem children. It is likely that Timmy's anger at and distrust of his early caregivers will be transferred to other substitute caregivers, and eventually to his teachers. If Timmy enters preschool at age three or four, he may be highly aggressive, withdrawn, or detached. In any case, he may not enjoy relating to his teachers, obeying them, listening to them, or learning from them.

As the demands grow on Timmy to concentrate in elementary school, his problems may multiply. Teachers may find Timmy to be "in his own world," to be nonresponsive. Or teachers may find him disruptive, hyperactive, and insatiable for attention.

And as Timmy senses the negative attitude of his teachers, it may confirm his early feelings of being unloved and unwanted. Self-esteem will suffer. He will most likely not have positive feelings about school and will have difficulty living up to his educational potential.

Melissa is another example of a child who later developed school problems. At two and one half months, she was enrolled in day care over 40 hours a week. She began her day at 8 A.M. and was not picked up until 5:30 or 6:00 P.M. This child-care arrangement continued until Melissa entered elementary school. At various times during her preschool years, it was reported by the center's staff that Melissa felt upset, angry, and fearful. It seemed to them that she longed to be home with her mother or father, especially in the afternoon hours. She grew resentful of her center teachers, and later this negative attitude carried over to her feelings about her elementary school teachers. Not surprisingly, it was hard for her to do well at school.

If Melissa's mother had been able to avoid 12-hour-a-day child care by working only part-time, Melissa might have been better able to avoid negative feelings and enjoy (or at least tolerate) her day-care experience. Of course, there are children in day-long child care who have positive feelings about their first institutional environment, and who do not begin elementary school with such negative attitudes. But if the day-care environment happens to be stressful or anxiety producing, and the child is unhappy during a large part of the day, this experience may influence later school functioning. To sum up, a negative day-care experience with staff, or with other children, or an impoverished environment can predispose a child to difficulty in elementary school.

Increased Risk of Delinquent Behavior

Teenagers who display antisocial personality disorder ("APD")—which is the same as psychopathic behavior—are responsible for a high percentage of delinquent behavior. They can be aggressive, reckless, thoughtless, mean, and act without remorse. As Magid and McKelvey explain: psychopaths "leave in their wake a huge amount of human suffering. The pain psychopaths wreak on other human beings can be physical, or it can be the mental anguish often felt by those who try to form relationships with them.

"Frighteningly, a growing number of individuals now being diagnosed as mentally ill fit this particular mental health category. These psychopaths comprise an increasingly large increment of the aberrant segment of our population. And they account for a disproportionate amount of deviancy."[28]

Magid and McKelvey go on to say that: "Many people with APD began life as unbonded, unattached children. Right now thousands of America's children are in danger of becoming unattached. Well-intentioned parents may be unknowingly placing their young infants at high risk.

We all know the stresses that modern life place on the family. Because of necessity or desire, more and more mothers are returning to work, many just weeks after the birth of their babies. Parents need to know that this may be putting their children at risk for unattachment."[29]

Stressful early childhood events may set the stage for delinquent behavior.

Emmy E. Werner reported in her study on "High Risk Children in Young Adulthood" that "more than half of the stressful life events that significantly increased the likelihood of having a criminal record or an irrevocably broken marriage by age 30 for members of this cohort took place in infancy and early childhood."

One set of events included "(unemployment of the major breadwinner, illness of the parent, and major moves) and having a mother who worked outside the home without stable substitute child care during the first year of the child's life.

A significantly higher proportion of males with a criminal record (including promotion of harmful drugs, theft and burglary, assault and battery, rape, and attempted murder) experienced such disruptions of their family unit in their early years."[30]

A few years ago, a desperate mother complained in my office that: by the time Sandra (her daughter) was 13 she had already been involved in shoplifting clothing and accessories from the department store at her neighborhood mall. In the past, there had been incidents of lying and stealing during her elementary school years. Sandra's working mother never truly confronted or dealt with these unpleasant issues because she wanted the few hours a day they spent together to be a pleasant and positive time.

When an infant, Sandra had been cared for by her parents until she was five months old. Then her parents separated and her mother, too depressed to cope with a baby, sent Sandra to live with her maternal aunt. After four months Sandra was reunited with her mother, but was cared for by a baby-sitter since her mother went to work every day. The child saw her father twice a month for her first two years, but those visits became less regular as Sandra grew to be a teenager.

Her mother described Sandra during her preschool years as a dependent, demanding, sensitive, and often irritable child. She treated her dolls and stuffed animals aggressively. Later, Sandra became more defiant and oppositional. If she was confronted at school with her lies and antisocial behavior, she showed little if any remorse.

Sandra is a good example of a child who had inconsistent care as an infant and was deprived of the chance to form a secure attachment with her mother. Commenting upon children with poor attachments or breaks in attachment, authors Magid and McKelvey, in their book *High Risk: Children Without a Conscience*, state that "the formation of a weak bond or a break in this attachment will lead to non-regulated discharge of a baby's energy, and mistrust and insecurity. Here lies the seed of antisocial personality disorder. This complicated and subtle pattern of interaction must occur between mother and child for a healthy attachment."[31]

When Sandra was older (five to eight) she seemed to have missed the optimum time period in which children learn to internalize values dealing with trust and respect for property. Basically, those are the critical years when children learn moral principles: tell the truth, do not steal, do not fight, behave responsibly to others. This transmission of values takes time, effort, and the ability to make sure the child is held accountable for any antisocial acts he or she commits.

Children like Sandra feel angry at the adults in their world perhaps because the significant adults were not "there" for them when they were infants. As a result, as teenagers they tend to look to other peers, or to "pop idols," as behavior models, and to accept their often less-desirable values. None of this is a conscious process. Yet all of it is a source of grief for parents who are often at a loss to understand why their school-age child or adolescent has so completely rejected their standards.

Obviously there can be other causes of antisocial behavior: parental divorce, abuse, the death of a parent, or other separations and losses that can disrupt an otherwise satisfactorily created bond. But regardless of such later traumas, bonding failures in the first two or three years of life alone can predispose the child and adolescent to aggressive actions and delinquent behavior.

As Magid and McKelvey state: "When an infant senses that its relationships with others have been disrupted and parental consistency is lost (as is frequently the case in unbalanced parental responsibilities in divorce), the infant is very likely to call forth a self-surviving instinct. This emotion is called rage. It is this rage and sadness that is at the core of the unattachment syndrome.

"This unresolved rage can simmer for years and manifest itself in a number of ways, ranging from antisocial criminal acts, to suicide, to abuse or neglect of their own children, perpetuating the cycle."[32]

Magid and McKelvey go on to suggest that "Our national spotlight should clearly be on the crib—not on the criminal—if we are to change the future. Infants who do not receive a warm welcome into the world will seek their revenge."[33]

Dr. Bowlby agrees, stating that "each of us is apt to do to others as we have been done by."[34]

Difficulty in Establishing Intimacy

According to psychologist Mary Ainsworth, the most important long-term result of the early failure to form a secure affectionate bond is the "inability to establish and maintain deep and significant interpersonal relations."[35]

In other words, infants and toddlers who do not have the chance to build a positive and secure emotional base, and who are thereby deprived of the opportunity to learn to trust and to love, are likely to have a problem reciprocating love. Thus, they are likely to have difficulties with relationships throughout their lives. The Carnegie Report tells us that "Substantial and consistent parental contact allows interactions that help the baby form secure loving attachments to parents

Children who have been deprived of love have difficulty experiencing love.

and other family members."[36] Another writer, Michael Rutter, observed that the absence of attachment may lead to what he called an "affectionless psychopath"—a personality characterized by a "lack of guilt feelings and an inability to form lasting relationships."[37]

Still another authority, pediatrician-author T. Berry Brazelton, says that "Unless a baby is allowed to experience fully these stages of trust and attachment, his or her ability to attach to important others will be either endangered or diluted."[38] Dr. Tiffany Field, a neonatal expert at the Mailman Center for Child Development in Miami, stated: "If you don't develop relatively harmonious interaction patterns early in life, you are going to have difficulty with peer relations and in social situations. We know that kids who have disturbed peer interactions are the ones most likely also to be delinquent or psychologically disturbed."[39]

When these emotionally scarred and deprived infants reach adolescence and adulthood, they are usually unable to make and keep an intimate alliance. Such an alliance, which might lead to marriage or a long-term commitment, is simply too threatening.

Speaking of men and women who never form secure attachments, noted child specialist Selma Fraiberg said: "Life histories of people with such a disease reveal no *single* significant human relationship. The narrative of their lives reads like a vagrant's journey with chance encounters and transient partnerships. Since no partner is valued, any one partner can be exchanged for any other; in the absence of love there is no pain in the loss."[40]

Marriage-and-family authority Philip Shaver similarly compared the link between an infant's first attachments with his or her parents, and his or her adult attachments with lovers and spouses. Shaver found that the parent-child attachment displays many of the same characteristics that a lover provides.

For example, when the parent creates a secure base the infant feels competent and thus senses that it is safe to explore the environment. As in adulthood, the lover who reciprocates our loving feelings similarly makes us feel confident, secure, and safe. But when this love partner acts uninterested, or rejects us, we feel anxious, preoccupied, unable to concentrate—just as an infant feels when the parent or caregiver is not available, or is not sensitive to the infant's needs.

When stressed, sick, or threatened, infants seek physical contact with parents or caregivers. Adults, when afraid, distressed, or sick, similarly seek to be helped and comforted by a lover or partner.

The parallel continues as Shaver describes various adult attachment types. For example, a securely attached lover would describe love as especially happy, friendly, and trusting, and be able to accept and support the partner despite his or her faults. Conversely, avoidant lovers would be characterized by fear of intimacy, by jealousy, and by emotional highs and lows. Anxious/ambivalent lovers experience love as involving obsession, a desire for reciprocation and union, emotional highs and lows, and extreme sexual attraction and jealousy.

Shaver also found that "both mothers and fathers play an important role in determining a child's long-term attachment style, and that both have the same kinds of effects." Shaver's subjects were asked to describe their parents as either caring, critical, intrusive, or responsive; their own attachment styles were then found to be much the same as those of their parents.[41]

As an adult, an insecurely attached person may not risk any intimate attachments because he or she learned as an infant to expect that those he or she cares about, and those who care for him or her may suddenly leave or be emotionally unavailable or unresponsive. As a child, he or she felt both loss and anger at those caregivers; self-image was damaged by the painful separations. No one wanted to stay, or to be protective or loving to such an infant.

Adult love relationships often parallel childhood experiences with parents.

Or, an adult may say, "I feel uneasy being close to others. I find it difficult to trust friends completely and difficult to allow myself to depend on them. I am nervous when anyone gets too close. Partners often want me to be more intimate, but I'm not comfortable with such intimacy."

But if this same person had experienced continuity of care as a child, and had been able to form a secure attachment, his or her adult relationships might be different. He or she might then say, as an adult, "I find it relatively easy to enjoy the company of others. I am comfortable depending on them and having them depend on me. I don't often worry about being abandoned, or about someone getting close to my heart." In other words, adult relationships often parallel childhood experience.

In commenting upon the lifelong consequences of deficient infant care, Harvard's Burton White states: "What's at stake is the basic human capacity for loving other humans."[42]

Perhaps the most disturbing conclusion was voiced by authors Magid and McKelvey, commenting upon the consequences of poor infant attachment: "In other words, the babies are at risk of becoming unattached and then never being able to experience the most important human emotion—love."[43]

Depression and Other Serious Mental Illnesses

"Depression" is a term widely used to describe an emotional state. In everyday language it means the depressed person feels sad, gloomy, perhaps without hope. Depressed people often find it hard to get out of bed in the morning. They feel a pervasive sense of pessimism. They are sometimes so immobilized they neither want to or cannot "do anything." They feel powerless and impotent. They may contemplate suicide, and in extreme cases some do kill themselves.

The intensity or degree of mental illness created by bonding failures depends upon several factors. These include the child's age, duration of these separations, and inherited predispositions. And, the younger the child when separations or losses are experienced, the more profound are the negative effects that predispose an individual to mental illness.

It is also true that the length of time the attachment figure is away from the child can seriously impact the child's mental stability. For example, if the mother is away only a few hours a day, the impact of the separation is far less than if a mother is absent from 7:30 A.M. to 6:00 P.M. five days a week.

In exploring the family history of many depressed patients, experts find that they have usually experienced significant childhood losses and disruptions. Consider the example of an infant whose parents left for most of the child's waking hours and who experienced a series of different caregivers. Such a child is more likely to experience sadness, depression, and anger. It is likely that he or she will feel unloved and unlovable. These feelings are much like those expressed by depressed adults.

Children deprived of positive nurturing experience in the *early* years also tend to be more vulnerable later to other kinds of mental ill-health than if they experience negative, anxiety-provoking events in *later* childhood, adolescence, or adulthood. Such events can include death or serious injury to one or both parents, parents' divorce, long separations from one or both parents, or separation from a long-term and beloved nonparent caregiver. Bowlby concurs and discusses how discontinuity of early attachments, as well as prolonged maternal deprivation, wrenching separations, or the unexpected death of an important attachment figure can, under certain circumstances, lead to serious disorders, including phobias, depression and psychopathic behavior."[44]

Cummings and Cichetti also agree with this view, stating: "children experience anxiety when separated from their primary attachment figure. In cases of prolonged or sustained loss, an intense mourning process follows. When this mourning process continues beyond a normal period of time, Bowlby views it as a reflection of an unresolved loss. Without the presence of a reliable internal working model, any loss will be experienced as paramount. Conversely, positive early experiences which result in good quality internal working models and loss may not be a devastating experience.[45]

Drs. Cummings and Cichetti offer other supporting evidence for the link between early losses (such as loss of caregiver) and mental illness. In discussing the effect of early attachment deficits, they say that "when these experiences occur early in life the notion that attachment figures will not be available when needed is likely to become a fundamental aspect of children's organization of personality, and to result in feelings and perceptions of insecurity that are resistant to change."[46]

They also point out that "insecure attachment and depression may not be separate developments, but are related occurrences that become evident at different stages in the child's life. Thus, insecure attachment might be observed initially in infancy and may be related to an increased risk of becoming depressed in the future."[47]

A study by psychologist T. W. Moore in 1969 of fifteen children who had experienced unstable and changing daily substitute care *before their second birthday,* found they were conspicuously insecure and anxious in their later years. According to their mothers, at age six these children showed excessive "dependent clinging behavior"; they wanted continuing physical contact and attention. Such negative behavior was also observed outside their homes when these children were at their child care center. As compared with other children, this group was more nervous and dependent and less able to adjust to events that occurred at the center. They were more fearful of "doctors and hospitals and the dark."[48]

Virginia Hunter, a psychologist, states in an interview with John Bowlby, "in my private practice I'm seeing more and more borderline children presenting at around age 7. More than, say, 10 years ago, and it seems to have some relation to the number of caretakers." In the interview, John Bowlby answers, "Oh yes, some of us have been aware of it for a long time."[49]

The borderline personality has extreme difficulty in his or her social relationships as well as in displaying appropriate emotional responses. These responses can be intense and explosive and at times unpredictable. It is difficult to treat these patients, as their needs are profound. Feelings of emptiness and exaggerated vulnerability to disappointments can trigger such unpredictable emotional responses. It is indeed hard to "fill up" their deep well of deprivation, and easy to fail at becoming the "perfect nurturer." A change in the time of appointment, for example, or a simple misunderstanding can produce enormous rage, withdrawal, or termination of treatment.

It is also true that therapists often have difficulty in treating either depression or other serious mental illness that is a result of these early preverbal losses. The patient usually cannot remember these early events or the important individuals involved. Furthermore, parents of the patient often do not

Frequent early losses can predispose a child to depression.

consider the lack of continuity for their infant and toddler significant and do not mention it either to the patient or to the therapist.

As a result, the patient's symptoms of sadness, sense of foreboding, and anxiety may persist without the roots of the problem ever being recognized or addressed even in a therapeutic situation.

It is obvious that if parents can minimize the frequency and intensity of loss experienced by infants, the future development of depressive and other psychological symptoms will be lessened.

So in summary, care given to infants and toddlers must be more than positive, nurturing, and compassionate. It must also have sufficient continuity to create an optimistic outlook on life so that the infant and toddler need not suffer the kind of loss and the feelings associated with mourning that so often is a significant cause of depression and other emotional illnesses.

Drug and Alcohol Abuse

Pervasive feelings of depression, inability to form close relationships, and a lack of ego satisfaction in their school experience add to the need for—and intensity of—an addiction to drugs or alcohol in adolescence. These negative factors are indeed interrelated, and these problems usually have their roots in bonding and attachment failures early in the life of the child (as well as the quality of the parenting they have received).

When young children feel that the adults in their life do not really care about them or nurture them, they tend to seek other ways to get pleasure and satisfaction. Children who have been deprived of secure adult attachments are more likely to find pleasure in food, their bottle, or their toys.

Addictive behaviors may have their roots in early childhood experience.

Consider Doris, who lived in the suburbs of an eastern city. She had five different caregivers by the time she reached the age of two. As we have pointed out, a child like Doris was unable to sustain a stable attachment. She felt repeatedly "abandoned" by her caregivers. To protect herself from painful feelings—disappointment, abandonment, and fear—she turned away from relationships with people and looked elsewhere for satisfaction. Where did she find it? Doris compulsively pulled, twirled, and tugged on her hair. When it grew long enough, she smelled and mouthed it.

Some of these children who had similar problems may suck their thumb constantly; some become headbangers; some masturbate excessively. These activities yield pleasure at will, pleasure they can control as desired. Other children may overeat, or withdraw from social contact and appear to be in their own fantasy world.

Ultimately, children who have found pleasure primarily from the bottle, from food, and from other autoerotic stimuli, may continue to find similar sources of pleasure as they grow older. During the stresses of adolescence they may begin to use more destructive and damaging substances like drugs and alcohol, or engage in promiscuous sexual behavior, which provides immediate gratification. These activities give them the same kind of tension release and pain reduction that, as toddlers, they got from their bottle, food, masturbation, or rocking.

Moreover, adolescents who in early childhood did not form a trusting bond with an adult, and who now cannot form affectionate ties with peers or important adults in their life, look for substitutes for the pleasures of personal relationships. These young people may also be more susceptible to drug and alcohol abuse. The pleasure and comfort derived from those substances can seem, to the teenager, more reliable than any reward that a personal relationship can offer. These adolescents may become "solitary" alcoholics, or "loners" who use drugs in the privacy of their homes. They appear to be in control of their own pleasure, and need not take part in dating, parties, or other normal social activities.

Nor is it likely that such adolescents will outgrow this unfortunate pattern of behavior. The probability is that many of them will continue, as adults, to have drug and alcohol problems. But the roots of those problems may be found in their infant/toddler years, when they were never given consistent and positive nurturing.

As psychiatrist John L. Weil states: "A chronic depletion of pleasure recorded during infancy, and triggered and amplified during adolescence, can contribute to the onset of alcohol addiction."[50] Weil also notes that adolescents "who had been severely deprived of empathic care during infancy run a statistically greater chance of manifesting alcohol dependency and addiction."[51]

Adolescents deprived of proper nurturing during infancy are more likely to become addicted to alcohol.

We have now briefly described five major social problem areas in which bonding failures seem to be a significant causal factor. But it is also true that in the years following infancy, diminished parental presence and supervision, divorce, death, illness, and other traumatic experiences play their part in aggravating these ills. Although we know that many individuals in our lives can provide inspiration, support, and protection, the practical truth is that for most of us, the parent is *the* person upon whom children rely.

No matter how nurturing the substitute caregiver, no matter how inspirational the teacher, and no matter how understanding the counselor or therapist, those positive relationships often are self-limiting and do not persevere into adulthood. And as those relationships come and go—even though they are positive and contribute significantly to the life of the child—the child is nevertheless continually subjected to a form of caregiver roulette. While the older child, who is verbal, can be prepared for such changes, even older children still feel a sense of sadness and loss when such relationships end.

Realistically, therefore, only the parent can be counted upon throughout the childhood years (and even into adulthood) to provide emotional security, intellectual stimulation, and an environment that is loving and joyful. As explained in Chapter 6, this kind of positive parental presence plays a most important part in helping the child avoid the social ills we have been discussing.

At all ages, throughout the entire period of childhood and even into adulthood, parental presence that is warm and responsive can represent an important stabilizing and therapeutic force. Parental presence alone may not automatically prevent some of these ills but without such continuity of care, future problems are usually more frequent and more severe.

Magid and McKelvey leave us with a final warning about caregiver roulette: "Never before in the history of the country have so many parents been away from home and their children at the most critical times." They also say "With so many mothers working, just who is taking care of the children? Proper bonding and attachment cannot occur when the infant's significant caregiver isn't around and the baby has no reliable, consistent, or loving substitute caregiver. Without suitable answers, these problems could result in a national attachment crisis, thus putting a future generation at high risk."[52]

> **Bonding and attachment crises could put future generations at high risk.**

Parental Versus Substitute Care:
A Comparison

In Chapter 4, we examined some of the long-term risks to the intellectual, emotional, and moral development of a child when he or she is subjected to frequent caregiver changes during the preverbal years. In Chapter 6, we will explore many of the special benefits that accrue to children as the result of consistent parental care during the preverbal years—and the continuing benefits of a parental presence during the later years of childhood. But before we do that, let us look at two examples of parental and substitute care that we may characterize as "adequate," "average," or "typical" and explore some of the differences between the two.

We are certainly aware that both parents and substitute caregivers differ greatly in warmth and responsiveness, and that even from day to day there can be variations in the ability of each to attune to the child. Nevertheless, we will try to describe two typical child-care situations with these differences in mind. One example describes a parent's day with her child. The other describes the life of a child with a competent, loyal substitute who is paid to care for the toddler of full-time, working parents.

There can be significant differences between these two kinds of "adequate" child care. To examine some of the differences in the quality of child care each situation offers, let us posit two scenarios.

Betty is an accountant in a large firm. Her husband, Robert, teaches mathematics in a suburban high school. Their daughter, Jane, age two is—so far—their only child. When Betty was pregnant she worked up to the last two weeks before delivery. She made sure she got competent prenatal care; and she prepared herself for motherhood by reading child-care books. Betty and Robert attended classes dealing with childbirth and infant care given at a local community center.

"I really wasn't trying to glorify motherhood or make myself into a perfect mother," says Betty. "All I wanted to do was enjoy my baby and give her a head start in life."

From the time Jane was born, Betty decided that despite the financial sacrifices involved, she would stop work and act as the primary caregiver for her daughter. She would "take the plunge," stay home, and be a full-time mother as long as she and Robert could manage it. When she took a leave of absence from her job she told her boss "I'll be back when Jane is about three; I hope there will be a place for me."

"Sometimes I'm not entirely thrilled about that decision," Betty says. "I love Jane and I want to see her develop and be there to help her grow. But I miss my work. I worry about my future in the firm. And there are many times when I feel bored, irritable, tired. But I made my choice and I intend to stick with it at least until Jane is three."

Betty is not a perfect textbook mother. She worries about Jane's eating habits and tends to pester her too much about them. Like most mothers, she gets "uptight" over some areas of childrearing yet is relaxed with others. However, she has a real desire to be a good mother.

Now let us meet Sally, a competent, affectionate, and compassionate nanny. She has been the primary caregiver for two-year-old Randy ever since his mom, Iris, returned to her job as a buyer when Randy was three months old. She has continued to take care of Randy while both of his parents work full-time. She wants to do her job well and most of the time, she does.

Randy has been lucky to have Sally care for him while his mom goes to work. Over the past nearly two years he has formed a close bond with Sally. He is able to depend upon her for comfort and security. He has grown into a trusting and cheerful child mainly because he has had the advantage of continuity of positive care with Sally. He has not been exposed to the experience of multiple losses from frequently changing caregivers; he has avoided caregiver roulette. Just as Jane has developed a secure attachment with her mother, Betty, so Randy has with Sally.

And just as Betty is not a perfect mother, Sally is not a perfect nanny. She has her good days and her bad days. She often feels guilty about not being at home when her own children, 12 and 13, get back from school. But she is reliable, efficient, and trustworthy. In other words, we may describe Betty as a good mother, and Sally as a good substitute caregiver.

> *Betty is not a perfect mother; Sally is not a perfect nanny.*

Although both women are providing positive care, and both have established strong bonds and a secure attachment with the child in their care, there are some significant differences between the kind of care they provide for their young charges. To highlight these differences, let us compare a more or less typical day in the lives of Jane and Randy.

JANE'S DAY

Generally, Jane greets each day optimistically. On this morning, she climbs out of her bed and into bed with her mother and dad. "Read me a book," she says. Her sleepy mother complies and reads to her. After the first rabbit story, Jane asks, "Where is Baby Rabbit's mommy and daddy?" To Betty, the child appears to be puzzled, perhaps even upset, because the fictional rabbit does not seem to have any parents. So Betty patiently explains that Baby Rabbit does have a mom and dad who love and take care of him—they just are not part of the story. Just then, a squirrel jumps up on the windowsill and looks in at Jane and her mother. Jane is excited at seeing the squirrel and asks Betty, "Why can't the squirrel stay in our house?" Betty again explains that "the squirrel needs to return to his family. He has a mom and dad who take good care of him, but now they are out looking for nuts and seeds to feed him in his own house in a hole in a tree." Jane smiles and seems pleased with her mom's explanation.

Except for a two-hour afternoon nap, Betty and Jane are together for most of the day. At times, Betty is doing household chores with Jane either underfoot or watching *Sesame Street*. Of course, during these moments, Jane may have to wait to have her story read or other needs met. Sometimes, Betty lies on the sofa observing Jane at play with her toys. At other moments, Betty will take the unexpected opportunity to teach Jane new words and concepts, either when looking at a picture book together or on a walk. For example, while riding to the market with her mother, Jane notices a construction site with a huge crane that is hoisting windows to be installed in a tall building. She excitedly points out the crane to her mother. Betty stops the car and they watch how the big machine picks up the heavy windows, and lifts them into the building. Later, at the park, they collect acorns and eat a snack together, swing on the swings and interact in a relaxed way.

After nap time, Betty asks a friend with another toddler to visit. The two children play near each other while the mothers watch, chatter away, and occasionally intervene when needed. Betty sets up a small table with some playdough on it, which keeps the toddlers busy for short intervals of time.

Although Betty does get tired at times during the day as Jane peppers her with questions, or may be suddenly oppositional and irritable, Betty tries to remain patient, to answer each question as best she can. Sometimes noisy power struggles occur and Betty feels frightened by her own rage. But most of the time, she enjoys Jane's curiosity, enthusiasm, and creativity. She is glad to see her slowly growing more independent, exploratory, and curious. She also tends to become critical and anxious if Jane does not live up to her expectations, and she creates a level of tension when Jane is demanding or negative.

Betty frequently manages to socialize with other mothers who have young children, although she notices that there are fewer mothers and more substitute caregivers at the park. She had also arranged to join a local "Mommy and Me" group when Jane was 18 months old. This was a group of other mothers with toddlers. The mothers spend every Tuesday morning discussing various aspects of child rearing.

They receive both support from each other and helpful guidance from the facilitator. This information was useful since Betty had little experience with children from her own past education and family.

Betty found that in addition to discussing childrearing and development in her Tuesday group, she also spent time on the phone chatting about child-care issues with other mothers and friends. At parties, or at the park with her friends, after discussing various current topics, she finds that they soon fall into familiar talk about kids and the problems in raising them.

Sometimes she thinks about the challenges and stimulation that she previously experienced at her job. But she also finds that the challenges of being a good mother utilize a large part of her creative energy and imagination. She enjoys the intimacies, gossip, and support obtained with other mothers who have made a similar decision to stay home temporarily as full-time mothers.

> **Betty finds that being a good mother is a challenge and hard work.**

Of course, there are times when Betty gets short-tempered and impatient with Jane; at those times she is not always so attuned to her questions and needs. Even so, Jane is learning to know her mom, to "read" her moods, and to anticipate her responses to her behavior. Betty, knowing that she "lost it" earlier when she acted cross and irritable, tries to compensate with an apology and an extra hug.

Betty also manages to take some time off away from home. Once or twice a month Betty and her husband manage to have dinner together or see a movie when Jane's grandmother can care for her. During the week she exchanges baby-sitting with another mother and her husband takes over one evening when she attends a class. Since these intervals are short, the separations help Jane develop a tolerance both for dealing with a new personality as well as having some special time with her dad. She also learns to cope with her mother's absence. For just as infants must learn to deal with new foods with different consistencies, so toddlers must gradually learn to deal with brief periods of separation.

Now let us compare Jane's day with her mother, with Randy's day with his caregiver, Sally.

RANDY'S DAY

Randy's mom, Iris, is a buyer for a major retail women's clothing chain. Her husband, Ed, is an elementary school principal. When Randy was born, Ed and Iris talked about the possibility of Iris quitting her job to stay with Randy. But they decided that it would be better, even for Randy, if Iris took only a brief maternity leave and returned to work after three months. The couple felt they needed Iris' income to pay the mortgage on their larger new home, to keep up the payments on their new station wagon, and to maintain the lifestyle they grew to enjoy before Randy was born: dining out frequently, entertaining, and taking weekend trips. Besides, Iris worried that if she stayed away from her job for longer than three months, it would hamper her prospects of being promoted to head buyer.

Randy's parents felt they needed two incomes.

Iris found other ways to explain her decision. For example, she felt she would be a better mother for Randy if she went back to work because of the stimulation she got from her job. Then too, she pointed out that the "quality time" she spent with Randy every evening and on weekends would be more than enough to make up for her weekday absence.

Iris was fortunate in finding Sally, a pleasant and affectionate woman, when Randy was three months old. Sally was 38 when she first started taking care of Randy, and her own children were then 10 and 11. Sally was an experienced caregiver and was highly recommended by previous employers.

On a typical day, Sally would arrive for work at 7:30 A.M. Iris was already up with Randy, giving him breakfast. "Read me a story, Mommy," Randy said.

Iris patiently explained that she had to get ready to go to work, and did not have the time to read to him "right now." But Randy was persistent. "Read me a story," he said and even handed his mom a favorite book.

When Iris again tried to explain that she was in a hurry to get ready for work, Randy began to cry in frustration. He knew what he wanted; he wanted his book read to him now; he did not want to wait. Iris impatiently told Randy, "You'll have to learn when I tell you 'no.'" Randy cried harder, and said, "Where's Sally, where's Sally?" Frustrated by his mother's refusal to read to him, Randy began to call for Sally, his nanny, with whom he had, by now, formed a very affectionate bond.

Just then Sally arrived, promptly at 7:30. Iris picked Randy up, handed him to Sally, and left the room to dress and make a hurried breakfast for herself and her husband. Meanwhile, Randy handed Sally his favorite book and demanded that she read it to him. Sally found a comfortable chair and held Randy on her lap. She was a pleasant woman with a grammar school education. Her English, though passable, was accented. She read the book to Randy, trying to be responsive and cheerful. It seemed to satisfy him. He stopped crying and listened attentively as he snuggled close to her. However, there was no verbal interchange concerning the story or the pictures once the story was over.

After Iris and her husband left for work in their separate cars, Sally began her day with Randy. It was warm, with the sun up early, so Sally suggested to Randy, "Let's go to the park," but before going, Sally decided to get a few of the household chores out of the way. She turned on the television and flipped the channels until she found a cartoon in progress. She put Randy in front of the television set.

After 45 minutes, when the beds were made and the dishes put into the dishwasher, she carefully buckled Randy in the stroller and headed for the park five blocks away.

On the way to the park, Sally met another caregiver who she had seen previously at the park. They walked together side by side, both pushing strollers. They chatted together enthusiastically. The children, also side by side, were quiet and seemed content. There was no discussion between the children and either caregiver.

The park had a sandbox, swings, and slides. Many children and their caregivers gathered there each day. A few of the infants and toddlers were with their mothers, but most in this middle-class neighborhood were like Randy, with their substitute caregivers.

Sally by now knew a few of the other caregivers, and they talked among themselves while the children played. For a while Sally put Randy on a swing and pushed him to and fro. Later Randy had a snack and then climbed on the toddler-sized jungle gym. Sally stood nearby, watching to make sure he did not fall, even while she continued to speak to the other nannies and baby-sitters. Here again there was little verbal communication between Randy and Sally, but Randy felt secure with Sally nearby.

When an older child took Randy's shovel, he began to wail. Sally stepped in, retrieved the shovel, and gave it back to Randy, who stopped crying. It was clear that he appreciated Sally's support. But except for this one responsive act, there was no other communication between the two.

Sally and the other caregivers continued their spirited discussions throughout the morning as they watched over their young charges.

At noontime, Sally put Randy in the stroller and they began the five block journey to Randy's home. As Sally pushed the stroller home, they passed by workmen fixing a deep hole in the street with a skiploader. Randy pointed to the noisy machine and said "truck!" Sally smiled at Randy, repeated the word "truck," and kept moving. She did not slow down or stop to explain to Randy what they had both seen.

At home, Sally fed Randy a pleasant lunch. Again, there was a minimum of discussion. She put Randy down for his nap with a song from her childhood.

When Randy woke up, she put him in the stroller and went to the local market to buy a few groceries for dinner (Iris had left her a short list). After the trip to the market, Randy played in his own sandbox while Sally watched quietly. Later in the afternoon, Sally turned on the television again and Randy watched cartoons. Then Sally gave Randy a snack and settled down next to him on the sofa. They watched the television together until Iris returned home from work at 5:30 P.M.

A COMPARISON: BETTY AND SALLY

These scenarios are two examples of "typical" child care. One is provided by the "good enough" mother, the other by a "good enough" substitute caregiver. Both Jane and Randy are securely attached to their primary caregiver: Jane to her mother Betty, and Randy to his nanny Sally. As a result, both children are able to reap the benefits of the continuity of positive care that furnishes them with their "secure base" (see Chapter 3).

But parents who are in a position to make the choice between working and staying home should understand that there can be significant differences between care by a parent and care by a substitute.

Betty is consciously interested in both the emotional and intellectual development of her child. She feels pleasure when she talks with Jane. As Betty identifies a squirrel, a tree, bird, or automobile for her toddler, and observes Jane's responses, she is gratified. Even though she is not communicating complex concepts, she is enjoying her child's ability to learn, and her inquisitiveness and willingness to experiment. In the evening she tells her husband special things about Jane's day. This reinforces Jane's feeling that she is valued since her mother seems to enjoy reliving Jane's experiences. She probably feels an enhanced sense of confidence, self-worth, and contentment. And all of this stems from one simple fact: her mom was "there."

On the other hand, the quality of the relationship between Sally and Randy, though positive, is not as intense. It is more "custodial." Sally, although pleasant and kind, may not have the same motivation required to expand Randy's range of interests, or to stimulate him. Sally feels her job is done—and done well—if she protects the child from injury, comforts him when he is unhappy, and cares for his physical needs. Except for the outdoor digging in the sandbox and the use of some of the park equipment, Randy's play was limited. While at home Sally did not provide him with blocks, puzzles, playdough, or wooden beads to string even though he had this equipment in his room.

Nor is Sally there in the evening to recount to his parents the events of Randy's day. She is not there to report the incident about the older boy taking Randy's shovel. Nor is she there to tell how the skiploader and construction workers were fixing the big hole in the street.

Randy cannot reminisce about his days with his mom and dad.

Randy is thus deprived of the important verbal reinforcements from his mother and father that would help him make sense of his experiences. He has no one with whom to reminisce at bedtime about the things that made him laugh, cry, or frightened. His mom and dad have no "window" into his day for a simple reason: *they were not there.*

Clearly, it is neither fair nor logical to expect even a nurturing caregiver like Sally to provide the quality of care comparable to that of a parent like Betty. It is one thing to protect a child from physical harm, and to comfort and feed him and return him safely to his parents at night. It is quite another to stimulate him, to teach him about the many things in his world, to foster his creativity, and to encourage a sense of joie de vivre.

It may not seem fair to make a comparison between Betty and Sally. Describing differences in caregiver behavior may seem elitist and it may appear to stress class differences. But the intent is not to be judgmental but to realistically describe current childrearing processes by two better-than-average caregivers. Unfortunately, most baby-sitters do not have training in child development. They have little if any supervision and few guidelines in dealing with television viewing, and so on. Many are also expected to include housekeeping duties as part of their jobs.

Still, many substitute caregivers nurture in ways that are positive, loving, and at times more appropriate than some parents. But even those who are devoted and have been with a family through many years may not have the interest or ability to convey ideas and concepts that serve to increase the child's understanding of the world or to help create a social conscience or special skills.

However, a motivated, loving, responsive parent can make a vast difference in a child's life. For one thing, children feel a greater attachment to their mother and father. In turn, the average parent feels a more intense investment in and commitment to the child: there is always the hard-to-define involvement due to the parental relationship as compared to a substitute. For another, parents are usually more motivated to provide a richer emotional and cognitive environment to stimulate their child. Putting it altogether, it seems clear that although Sally *is* an excellent substitute, the care that is provided by Betty has profound long-term advantages for her toddler. The reason for the difference can be summed up as that irrational involvement that we may define as "parental love."

Why Parental Care is Worth It

Looking back at the life history of most successful adults, one is struck by their remarkably similar early attachment experiences. During both early and later childhood years, the adults in their lives—usually at least one parent—provided not only continuity of positive care, but also inspiration and emotional support. Let us then examine in more detail some of the benefits—both predictable and unexpected—that flow from the parental decision to undertake the role of primary caregiver during the earliest years, as well as a supervising and involved caregiver during the later years of childhood. As we will see, such parental involvement has lifetime implications. As the Carnegie Report states:

Most successful adults had a supportive relationship with at least one parent.

"Infants' early experiences with adult caregivers also provide the building blocks for intellectual competence and language comprehension. Touching, holding, and rocking a baby as well as stimulating the child through talking and reading seem most effective for later development. When parents perform these behaviors in a responsive and attentive manner, they foster their child's early cognitive competence in ways associated with later academic achievement, work performance and social adaptation."[1]

While the first chapters of this book deal with a lack of continuity in the early years, older children also need motivated and consistent care, in both the preschool period and later in the afterschool hours. These hours account for a significant part of the older child's daily life. At all times and at all ages, the child can benefit in countless ways by the presence and involvement of a caring parent who responsibly participates with the child through play, reading, supervision, accountability, and other interactions.

The first of these periods is the time from birth to about age two when most children acquire language ability—to both speak and understand, and to form secure attachments. This subject is covered in detail in Chapters 2, 3, and 4. As I explain in those portions of this book, I feel that this preverbal period has received far too little attention.

The second of the periods involves older children with language ability. And it is truly amazing how the cognitive and language abilities of young children seem to escalate almost daily. Intellectual development is dependent upon the adults who are present in the lives of these children. Of great importance is how each individual (parent and others) stimulates, educates, and interacts with the child. Now we will consider how parents can enrich both the emotional and cognitive environments of children after they become verbal, at approximately age two.

Once the preschool and school years begin, and children spend more time in school settings, parental time requirements are reduced. Though parents can feel more comfortable returning to work, they still should make every effort to be there when children return home from school. These afterschool hours offer parents a special opportunity to support the special interests, abilities or gifts of their children as well as deal with their problems and handicaps. In nursery school, kindergarten and the primary grade years, this may require hands-on personal involvement. But as the years progress into adolescence, the character of afterschool involvement changes from a hands-on presence to the more discreet role of supervisor, observer, and chauffeur.

Language and Cognitive Development

As compared to substitutes, parents are usually more intensely motivated to enrich their children's life experiences through verbal interaction. This can take the form of the parent echoing verbal responses of infants. The pleasure both parent and child share in sounds, rhythms, and melodies provides enrichment. For example, four-month-old Amanda may

Brain development that takes place in the first year is more rapid and extensive than previously realized.

say, "oo"; her mom can respond, "oo-oo-oo," changing the rhythm while repeating the sound. This is, as we have noted, part of the bonding process and the early beginnings of language. As time goes on these sounds will evolve into meaningful words, symbolic of objects, ideas, and feelings. It may be difficult to accept the fact that the first year of life is so important to the learning process. But as the Carnegie Report states, "Brain development that takes place before age one is more rapid and extensive than we previously realized."[2]

This developmental process continues in the second year of life. Cognitive growth and language development escalate exponentially as toddlers are exposed to more complex experiences and the nervous system matures. Simple songs and phrases slowly increase language ability; simple phrases like "all gone," repeated with melodic cadence, provide pleasure for the child and at the same time communicate concepts such as an empty glass, bottle, or dish.

A parent who is "there" also has the opportunity to interpret experiences for the child. Such opportunities can be used effectively in the second year of life, particularly as the child acquires the ability to understand words. Many everyday experiences, both visual and auditory, allow an interested and alert parent to provide cognitive and language stimulation.

Watch Sarah, for instance, as she walks with her two-year-old son Jeremy to the park. She may point out a fire engine or a moving truck or a motorcycle. She may say, "There goes a noisy fire engine. The firefighters are riding on the fire engine.

They are going to put out a fire." Later that evening Sarah can tell father, with Jeremy present, that "Jeremy saw a noisy fire engine go by." So the child has not only experienced the event, but later reintegrates the experience as it is discussed. The incident can also be retold or played out at various times during the week with blocks, cars, dolls, and other play equipment. Children enjoy hearing over and over again about experiences they have had. This repetition and reinforcement not only helps them develop their own language, but also to understand what they have experienced. Small events, such as "the fire engine racing by," may occur many times. Each one gives a parent the opportunity to communicate with the child and help him or her make sense of the experience.

For example, mother or father can explain to Jeremy that "the loud noise from the fire engine"—which may have scared him—"tells the other cars to get out of the way so the fire-fighters can speed to the fire. The ladders on the fire truck help the firefighters climb into high places. The hoses on the fire truck carry water to put out the fire." In effect this simple, single event gives the parent an excellent opportunity in the following days to educate and stimulate Jeremy. Depending upon Jeremy's interest, his parents can use this same example to explain that other vehicles such as ambulances, police cars, and some trucks, also go fast, have sirens, and make loud noises. Jeremy's play can also reflect his experiences and this, in turn, can reinforce his language development.

If a parent is not there to share the event, this kind of reinforcement and teaching may not occur. There is no practical way for the parent to know what the child has seen or enjoyed, or what may have frightened the child. It is less likely that a substitute caregiver would have the motivation (and perhaps not even the language ability) to use such an event as an opportunity for cognitive stimulation. More to the point, it is impractical—perhaps almost impossible—for the average substitute caregiver even to try to tell a parent, in the evening, what excited, alarmed, frustrated, or enraged the child during the day. As a consequence, reinforcement through discussions and play of significant events may never take place.

If the mother is present during most of the day, language stimulation is usually greater. The child will hear her voice talking on the telephone, chatting with neighbors, or at the local market as well as direct communication to the child. This reinforcement and repetition of speech is essential for language learning. As linguistics professor Dr. Naomi Baron explains in her book *Growing up with Language:* "Language learning emerges out of the language duet between adult and child that begins in the early months of life."[3] She also states: "Engaging toddlers in conversation, even one-sided conversation, is the most important thing you can do to nourish your child linguistically—structure your conversation as if your child is intelligent, listening to what you are saying, and understanding."[4]

> *Reinforcement and repetition of speech is essential for language learning.*

A mother also may be motivated to listen carefully to her child so she can interpret his or her early sentences. Most of us know how hard it can be to understand what a toddler is saying, or to understand the simplest of the child's communications. But a parent who is intimately involved with the child every day is usually able to pick up rudimentary verbal cues and interpret what the child is trying to express. As poet Francis Palgrave said over 100 years ago, in "Love's Language," "Their little language the children have, on the knee they sit: And only those that love them can find the key to it."[5]

Obviously, if the daily substitute caregiver speaks little or no English, nourishment in the English language will usually be at a minimum. However, foreign speaking caregivers can stimulate the child verbally by using their own language, expressions, and songs. It is also true that the substitute would not have the ability to pick up clues or be otherwise attuned to the infant's attempts to develop facility in English. And this is clearly the case even with the most motivated of nonparent caregivers.

For example, a two-year-old may want to use a tool like a toy hammer but not be able to convey this message. He may say "knock, knock," instead of "hammer." It is necessary to focus on the child's primitive communication and learn what it is that he or she is actually saying. The parent can be responsive to the request by saying, "Oh, you want to use the hammer and go knock, knock, don't you?" The parent goes to the toy shelf, locates the hammer, and supervises while the child "knocks" the wooden pegs with the hammer. At this moment, the child not only learns a new word—"hammer"—but also feels the parent cares about what he or she is trying to say, and what he or she wants.

The parent who models responsiveness when the child verbalizes is also teaching the child something else that is valuable: to listen to and ultimately respond to what the parent requests. Many parents complain that "My child won't listen to me." They are

Why some children will not listen to parents.

often irritated and impatient at the child's seeming lack of attentiveness. Parents may not understand that a child first must want to listen. This process has several parts.

It begins when the human voice brings pleasure to the child through a song, a story, a whisper, funny sounds, or other noises made by the parent: the "moo" of a cow, the "neigh" of a horse, a lullaby, or a folk song. The child who enjoys pleasurable sounds will feel that it is worthwhile to listen to the human voice. It is, in a way, similar to an adult who enjoys listening to a favorite television or radio program. If the programs merely reminded us of our chores and responsibilities, few of us would bother turning on the set. The child learns to listen when the sound of the parent's voice contains something that the child enjoys hearing. This is how learning and responsiveness is developed. Parental speech should not be limited to prohibitions, demands, criticisms, and announcements of chores but should offer much that is joyful and fun to hear.

Another facet of the process requires the parent to take sufficient time to listen to the child and respond to what he or she says. This obviously is time consuming and not likely to happen to families during the hurried comings and goings of the day. It is a process, therefore, that best takes place when there is freedom from time pressure, and when the parent is not in a rush to put the child to sleep and get on to other "important" chores. Moreover, learning occurs best in conjunction with the bonding process. The child who has positive feelings, who feels a secure attachment, wishes to please the parent and is thus more likely to respond to the parent's requests. This relationship helps motivate not only the learning of language, but also the internalization of social and disciplined behavior.

Mealtimes provide another excellent occasion to help the child develop language and social skills. One of the advantages of having the parent present during meals is that it gives mother or dad a priceless opportunity to use language in a relaxed and positive atmosphere, and is a good time for the child to connect the parent's words with the pleasures of feeding. The baby gets satisfaction from food and from the sound of the parent's voice. The simple naming of objects, and expressions such as "all gone" or "eat your carrots," "here's your blue cup," "hold your spoon," and so on are typical and appropriate mealtime phrases. Recently I observed an excellent, very well-equipped, and competently run day-care center. I was struck by how few words were spoken to the infants or toddlers by the caregivers. The communications that I did hear were between various staff members. What I missed hearing was a playful verbal interchange that often occurs between parents and children. (It is, however, possible that staff personnel were self-conscious with an observer present.)

Ability to Understand Children's Fears

To really know their child, parents must understand the child's fears and anxieties. It is important to realize that while some of children's concerns are developmental, most are caused by specific frightening experiences.

Consider the story of Mary, age two, who is brought to a supposedly excellent day care center at 8:00 A.M. by her working mother. An hour later Mary accidentally walks behind another child swinging on a playground swing and is hit by the moving swing. Mary is knocked down and frightened, but she is not really hurt. Mary cries while being comforted by one of the child-care workers. Twenty minutes later she is again playing with other children.

Mary's mother picks her up at her usual 6:00 P.M. but is told nothing about the incident. This is not a criticism of the child-care center. The caregivers who discharge the children in the evening may be different ones from those who care for children in the morning. Furthermore, there is no reason to assume that such "minor" incidents would be discussed in the few hurried minutes of pickup by parents rushing on their way home from work to fix dinner.

That evening, however, Mary's mother is puzzled by the child's irritability. The next morning Mary's mother is still puzzled, and may feel upset or even angry when Mary says, "I don't want to go to the center today. I want to stay home. I'm afraid."

The mother does not have a clue as to why Mary suddenly resists to going to the center. A power struggle may occur. Mary may feel that her mom and dad are not protecting her because she feels they are sending her into what she feels is a "scary" situation. Unfortunately, she is not able to tell her parents why she is afraid. Mary's mother is at her wit's end. The center is expensive and fees must be paid whether Mary goes or stays home.

Mary's mother does not understand Mary's behavior.

Furthermore, mother has an important meeting at work that day. So Mary is told she must go to the center; she is taken there despite her protests. Now Mary feels angry and misunderstood. And all of this comes to pass because Mary's mother did not—could not—know what happened. *She was not there.*

If the same event had occurred when Mary's mother was with the child at the park or playground, or if Mary had sufficient language ability to report her concern, the entire incident would probably have been handled differently. For example, as Mary's mother comforted the child, she could explain: "Mary, it is dangerous to walk behind a swing. I'm sorry you were knocked down and frightened."

Several hours later the same day Mary's mother could again talk about the incident: "You didn't like it when the swing hit you today, did you? Well, you have to remember to be careful when you walk behind the swings."

In the evening, the incident can once more be discussed with daddy or grandma. Eventually, Mary begins to understand what happened. Talking about such an event can help Mary put such incidents behind her. Moreover, it comforts Mary to know that her parents try to understand and be sympathetic when she is sad, or afraid, or in pain. And if Mary does seem fearful when returning to the park, her mother will know why. She might say, "We won't go near the swings today. We'll play in the sandbox instead. Maybe we can try the swings again next week."

The lives of our children are replete with countless such "small" events. Some are joyful, some painful, some interesting, some educational, some frustrating, some traumatic. Taken together, they comprise the life of our children. Yet in the 50 or so hours that working parents are away from their children each week, they are deprived of knowing about a significant number of these small happenings. In a way it is similar to spouses going on separate vacations, with each having experiences of which the other is ignorant. And though adults can discuss these events in some detail, not being on the scene deprives them of the total impact of the humor, fear, or other emotions evoked by them.

Parents don't usually get much information from substitute caregivers about the many small events that occur when parents and children are separated. But parents may ask: "Are not evenings and weekends sufficient, as a practical matter, to furnish me with enough mutual experience so I can know what is going on with my child?" Of course these hours together are valuable. But they are so limited that a parent may

Working parents are not aware of many small events that the child experiences.

not be able to understand and make sense out of the child's overall behavior. Many working mothers who bring their children in for therapy can report little in the way of the specifics when asked to describe their child's history. For example, these mothers are not aware what their child experienced in the park. They do not know if the child was disciplined or why they were disciplined. They do not know what they have seen on television. They do not know if they were frightened, why they were frightened, or if they fell, or were threatened with abandonment. All these problems may occur whether the child is in "day care," or "family care," or even at home with a nanny. However, the "at home" parent has a valuable window into most of the child's daily experiences. Therefore, when the child's behavior does become of concern, and the child is fearful and anxious, most such parents can help the therapist reconstruct the events and history to aid in the therapeutic process.

Being There to Aid in Other Developmental Growth Experiences (Giving Up Diapers, Bottles, Pacifiers, and so on)

In our culture, toddlers and preschoolers are expected to stop using diapers and begin to use a toilet. Also, during these early years, parents demand that breast-feeding and/or the use of a bottle give way to cup and glass. Pacifiers become "no-no's" in many households in the third year of life. Most parents expect these developmental changes to take place at any time from 18 months to four years of age. But during this same period the child's sense of self is emerging, and he or she may become increasingly negative and oppositional.

Toilet or potty training can be considered a unique challenge, as it is the child and not the adult who has control of his or her body. The young child must be taught and motivated to both hold back his or her bowels or urine, as well as to relax and release them at the appropriate place. It is certainly *not* a simple task, either for child or parent, to master this physiological process. It takes time, effort, patience, and even a bit of humor. Many adults feel frustrated by this challenge, and as a result many bring to the process their own anxieties and attitudes. In any case, it is important that the parent or caregiver determine:

- if the child can understand and is prepared for what is expected when the potty is introduced;
- that the child has words for urination and bowel movement;
- that the child is reasonably free of stress when toilet training is begun;
- that the child is neither shamed, denigrated, or humiliated if toilet training goes too slowly;
- that the caregiver avoids overreacting with anger at the child's first failures; and
- that the caregiver avoids showing disgust at the child's excrement or urine. There should never be a comment such as "You smell" or "You're dirty and stinky."

What is the emotional climate surrounding toilet training or giving up the bottle?

When a child does gain control and learns to use the potty, or stops demanding a bottle, he or she can feel both pride and pleasure in mastering these developmental milestones. But what kind of climate facilitates this learning process? Parents who are absent, or available only early in the morning or in the evening, may not be aware of how their substitute caregiver is handling these tasks. How intense are the power struggles that may occur? What techniques are used to motivate the child? Is he or she threatened, bribed, or spanked? Does the caregiver frighten the child, or become angry, or tell the child "grow up" or "don't be a baby"? Is the caregiver too indifferent or too tired to help the child take these new steps?

It is also true that some preschool centers will not accept the child who is still in diapers. As a result, the parents may speed up the process of toilet training and place added pressure on the child before the child is ready.

Giving up the bottle, diapers, or the pacifier may not be as simple or as easy as we hope. But when caregivers teach what is now expected of the child in a loving atmosphere, these achievements become growth steps that enhance the child's sense of self.

In all these developmental transitions, a parent who is *there* is in a position to know what is happening and to see how the child is reacting. In the case of toilet training, a parent can provide water, clay, dough or sand to allow some "messy" play while trying to help the child control his or her sphincters. If the child is giving up sucking on a breast, bottle, or pacifier, the parent can provide more cuddling, snuggling, and holding to help in the transition period, or provide other objects to mouth or chew on to replace the oral pleasures that are being denied. One mother planned an informal celebration to recognize the saying of "good-bye" to the pacifier.

Finally, a motivated parent who is *there* can at least know the emotional climate in which these developmental steps are being experienced. Even though the parent may not always deal with the changes in an ideal manner, he or she is more likely to be able to understand the power struggles that develop as a result of those developmental changes.

Diminishing Aggression and Sibling Rivalry by Parental Presence

"Why is it that as soon as I walk in the door, after a hard day away, complaints, wails, and screams erupt? My image of our happy home is shattered," Susan complains. "Our home seems to have become a verbal and physical battlefield. The rivalry between our two children can be as subtle as a look or a gesture, or as violent as a kick or a punch." Susan knows the situation demands attention, and cannot be ignored. "I don't know anything that makes me madder," she continues, "than when Sarah attacks our toddler."

Another mother complains: "My older boy constantly acts like a baby, whines, won't play by himself, tugs at me all the time. It's worse than having two babies! I feel like a rotten mother when I see my children so angry at each other, or the older one acting so immature. Why does my baby-sitter say they get along fine when I'm gone?"

Even parents who *are* home have a hard time remembering the moments when their children play together cooperatively, when one will teach the other something, or be supportive, kind, and sympathetic. True, for most children, the time spent in harmonious play outweighs time spent fighting and behaving aggressively toward each other. But what sticks more in our memory are those times when aggression erupts between siblings.

Sibling rivalry, as well as feelings of jealousy and envy, are basic human emotions. These feelings need to be identified and respected as powerful forces in the child's daily life and development. Rivalries and jealous feelings emerge even before a new baby arrives. These powerful emotions arise from the basic attachment and bond formed between child and parent (actually between any two individuals who have developed a loving relationship). The closer the bond, the more intense is the jealousy generated by the threat of an "intruder." Jealousy is a natural emotion. Depending upon its intensity, it may define the closeness of the basic attachment. For example, we would wonder about the strength of a marriage if one partner did not care if the other went out on dates with the opposite sex! Any activity that focuses on a thing, another person (including a child), or another activity, can arouse jealous and rivalrous feelings. In a sense a triangle is formed when:

- a mother and father engage in a rapt conversation that excludes the child;
- the parent is engrossed in a telephone call, a magazine or a book, a project, a sport, or a hobby; or
- the parent pays attention to other persons, either children or adults.

It is understandable that when a parent who is away all day first steps through the door in the evening, each child demands attention. Creating a squabble among themselves cannot fail to involve the parents—and thus get the desired attention. The intensity of rivalrous feeling is aggravated if each child feels deprived, tired, or hungry.

What makes it so difficult for parents is that each child needs something different. The infant may cry to be rocked and soothed. The three-year-old needs help building a block tower. The 18-month-old wants to splash in the tub. The five-year-old demands a book be read. All this goes on at the same time that dinner must be made, the house picked up,

> *At the end of the day, each child needs something different.*

the groceries put away. But if parents can devote more time and effort to each child every day, and provide developmentally appropriate experiences and play materials, they can help diminish the aggression associated with sibling rivalry. What also helps is arranging what I call "special time."

PROVIDING "SPECIAL TIME" FOR EACH CHILD

When a parent is available during most of the child's waking hours, he or she can create "quality time" for the child by providing what I call "special time." By this I mean time the parent sets aside or schedules to be alone with each child. This special time need not be long—twenty minutes may be sufficient if done regularly. This short period is under the child's control; he or she decides how to use it. The child may want to play, talk, hear a story, take a walk, be held or rocked, or have a snack. Or the child may want the parent simply to watch the child play, draw, or build. This can be a time for the child to express his or her feelings, fears, worries—to generally "unload." The parent can discuss some of the difficult events of the week, such as problems with siblings. Interruptions from the phone, other children, or adults should not be permitted. This will help assure the child that mom or dad respects this special time and will not allow any intrusion. This is a time for the child alone—no one else.

It is also important that special time is agreed upon, announced, and identified beforehand, both to the child and the rest of the family. Parents often assume that when they have spent time alone with the child, that was special time. But if the child is not aware of it as it occurs, he or she may not appreciate it. A parent may announce "Bobby will have his special time after his afternoon snack and Nancy will have hers before her bath tonight.

The value of this special time is that it says to the child: "I want to be with *you*. This time is special to me, too. You are important to me and I am interested in being with you, watching you play, and hearing about your activities. I am with you so I can listen to you, learn about your feelings, and be close to you."

Providing special time says, "I want to be with you."

When there is more than one child in the family, it is easy to treat the children as a unit or group, especially when they are close in age. This constant "togetherness" may intensify the rivalrous feelings between children vying for adult attention. But scheduling special time with each child is like someone being asked for a date by a valued person—it gives one a lift and makes one feel appreciated.

Facilitating Play: Painting, Water Play, Mud, Sand, Clay, Blocks, Dolls, Stuffed Animals, Dress-Up, and Dramatic Play

Clearly a lot of planning and preparation is involved in making a rich and appropriate play environment available to a child, not only to provide play materials, play opportunities, and supervision, but also to establish the secure base so that the child feels free to concentrate on play. The intensity and level of play is profoundly affected by the child's emotional state. If a child is worried or fearful or sad, the energy and motivation available for play decreases. If a child is angry, play may become destructive and aggressive and cannot be sustained.

An appropriate play environment demands planning and preparation.

If both parents work full-time, and the child does not yet feel comfortable with the baby-sitter or day-care arrangement, the quality and level of play will be diminished and less effective. Substitute caregivers may be reluctant to report lowered levels of play. Indeed, they may be pleased if the child spends extensive amounts of time in front of the television or napping in bed, making less work for the caregiver.

When parents return home in the evening the child often will display a noticeable spurt of energy, and want to play actively with them. Unfortunately, this spurt of play energy comes just when the tired working parents want such activity to wind down. This can sometimes lead to a power struggle: the child wants to play, the parents fervently wish he or she would quiet down and go to bed. But this is the first time all day that the child feels secure with mom and dad home; he or she has the energy either to play or to loudly protest if the parents are "too tired" to play. A parent who does not work away from home all day is likely to be more available, more motivated, and more energetic and therefore more willing to engage in a reasonable amount of play other than at bedtime.

Substitute caregivers tend to be far less likely than parents to play with infants and toddlers (as we have seen in Chapter 5). We are all familiar with a common scene: substitute caregivers walking with their young charges strapped into strollers while they spend the time chatting with other caregivers. Not only is there little verbal interchange; there is little or no eye contact between the substitutes and the infants or toddlers. Usually the child will be facing in the same direction as the substitute, which further cuts down both verbal and eye contact.

On the other hand, mothers are more likely to set up age-appropriate play environments that include considerable physical, verbal, and visual interactions. Most likely mother will invite other children to join in the play, providing important social experiences for the toddlers and preschoolers. Substitute caregivers and baby-sitters are understandably hesitant to take on the extra work and responsibility involved in such "play dates."

Kevin is two and a half years old. His mother, Jennifer, arranges for Kevin to have "play time" with friends like Joel who lives a block away. Joel's mother Susan frequently brings Joel to Kevin's home where both mothers supervise their play. There is sand, climbing equipment, and a table with play-dough and paints, all of which the boys enjoy while their mothers chat. If the play becomes too aggressive or unsafe, the mothers are available to intervene. At times the mothers will withdraw and encourage the children to play together by themselves. But, while parents should not necessarily intrude into their children's activities, they *can* help to set up a safe and stimulating play environment. It is also helpful to provide a play environment at a time when parent and child have the energy to deal with it. This is hard at the end of a working day.

It may be difficult for parents to understand how important play is to children. Yet it is through play that children primarily learn to understand and master their world. It is profoundly important for the quality of the child's life to have age appropriate activities. Children's play involves risk taking, experimentation, role-playing, the building and disassembling of objects, fantasy, and social interaction with both peers and adults.

Parents may not be aware of how important play is for children.

The child who plays constructively and creatively learns well. When play is treated with the same respect and dignity we accord important adult work, self-esteem is enhanced and the child gains pleasure, mastery, and good feelings.

The child's ability to play is helped by an environment that includes appropriate materials and equipment. Children normally do not need adult interaction or adult stimulation in their play. They do require some supervision to keep them safe, especially if the children are playing outdoors, or in an open, unfenced area. Safety is always the prime consideration whenever children play. This is particularly important when the child is involved with tools, cooking activities, and some forms of water play.

Child's play is not always what we adults think of as "play." An example of play might be a one year old dumping spoons from a drawer, a four year old wielding a "lance" fantasizing he is a knight in armor, a two year old squeezing and pounding playdough and experimenting with the texture and feel of this malleable material, an 18 month old climbing up and down steps; or a three year old using blocks to construct a high building and then knocking it down. The responsive parent will provide a variety of play equipment to facilitate such activities, both inside and outside the home.

Watching children at play can reveal to a parent a segment of the child's world. When children play, they often also talk. Therefore play not only develops both small and large muscle motor skills, but also facilitates the use of verbal interchange which can be amusing, enlightening and revealing. For the toddler and young child, certain play materials can be

Water, clay and paint should be part of every child's play experience.

tension reducers. For example, water play, mud, sand, clay, and finger paints are all wonderful materials for this age, but all require supervision. Preschoolers cannot yet set their own limits, so an adult presence is required. Otherwise, the play degenerates into an irritating mess. Yet the use of intrinsically messy materials should be part of every child's play experience. Arranging this kind of play does take more parental time and energy, but a child at this age should not be deprived of these experiences just because they demand more parental involvement. During these years the preschool child is learning bowel and bladder control and learning to control hitting, kicking, biting, and spitting. Play with water, sand, mud, and clay used in acceptable arenas provides expression of the kind of behavior that must be controlled in other areas.

BLOCKS

Blocks offer another important play experience that allows children to build, destroy, rebuild, and experiment. The child learns size and spatial relationships. Numbers are mastered through hands-on experience so that the concepts of quantity can be felt, seen, and talked about during block play.

Putting away blocks and other manipulative toys (beads and so on) provides opportunities for number concepts, sorting, and classifying. "Make piles of three." "Hand me all the square blocks." "Let's put away the triangles next."

Children develop a sense of parts and wholes; two smaller blocks equal the larger block; two similar triangles make a square or rectangle. This kind of learning combines visual, tactile, and verbal stimuli as well as experiences of balance. During this kind of manipulative play, small muscle coordination as well as cognitive skills are honed and sharpened.

Blocks are good for the creation of different environments for dramatic play. For example: a long highway for cars to be moved on; a corral to enclose the animals; a house, office, or store. Children usually verbalize while playing, thus reinforcing what they are learning about their world. Parents can encourage this by saying, "Tell me about what you are building." "Where are the animals going?" "Who lives in the house?"

Parents are not essential to the process of block play, but if they join in the play it can be a way of increasing verbal skills and vocabulary. Talking about the child's creations is an excellent way to have a truly child-centered conversation that is not involved with getting the child through the details of the day. ("Time to get dressed." "Lunch is ready." "Hurry up for school.")

With blocks, children will often play out frightening or upsetting incidents. They can be encouraged to act out such stressful events—car accidents, trips to the doctor or hospital—by recreating the scene with blocks and other props.

One of the problems with blocks, and with play materials that have many parts, is the irritation and stress that can arise in the "putting away" process. Preschoolers do not yet have the capacity independently to put away blocks and toys. They need some help. When cleanup becomes too much of a struggle, children will begin to avoid playing with these materials, and therefore be deprived of the rich benefits that blocks, and other sets with

When cleanup becomes too tedious, the child will stop using play equipment.

multiple pieces, have to offer. It should not be surprising that substitute caregivers might structure a child's play in order to avoid mess or disorder, or to avoid the work involved in putting these materials away. But parents who understand the value of block play can acknowledge that preschoolers need supervision and help in the job of putting things away, just as teachers provide structure and direction in preschool. Teachers schedule time for cleanup work, and treat it as an important part of the classroom day. Parents can structure the task by saying, "Joe, you hand me the blocks and I'll put them on the shelf (or vice versa)." This teamwork makes for a positive, cooperative atmosphere instead of a nagging power struggle. By scheduling enough time and supervision, and realizing that putting toys away is a mutual responsibility, the parent pays respect to the dignity of the child's play and play materials. Moreover, this approach to cleanup and "putting away" creates expectations in the child for order and organization. This will serve children well later on in school and will help build a constructive framework for future play and work.

So with block play, as with the other play activities, we see once again how essential are the motivation, energy, and patience of the truly involved supervising adult. As we have said before, in most cases such patience, motivation, and cognitive input are more likely to be supplied by a caring parent than by a substitute.

DOLLS AND STUFFED ANIMALS

Dolls and stuffed animals help children integrate and practice what they are learning about their world. Both boys and girls should have access to dolls and stuffed animals as objects for dramatic play and fantasy, for the release of aggression, to practice verbal skills, and as objects for comfort and cuddling.

Dolls and stuffed animals certainly help the preschooler when a new baby arrives in the household. Dolls can be fed, bathed, hugged, strolled, spanked, thrown, and drowned.

Preschoolers, whose verbal skills are still rudimentary, need the freedom to express all sorts of feelings they may have toward their sibling through play with dolls and stuffed animals. Preschoolers also need a safe way to express anger and aggressive feelings, since it is unacceptable to hit, kick, throw, bite, or spit at playmates or siblings. Some children use dolls as they would a playmate, creating an imaginary friend to talk to and boss around.

Dolls and stuffed animals are also helpful when parents want to communicate an important new idea to the child, or prepare or rehearse him or her for a new experience. They also help to reenact experiences that were difficult for the child, to clarify and make the upset more comprehensible. Talking directly to a child often does not work; the child may be "tuned out," or "won't listen." But the child usually is intrigued and captivated by listening to a doll, hand puppet, or stuffed animal "talk" (with the parent, of course, actually doing the talking).

Children will listen to their dolls and stuffed animals, but will "tune out" their parents.

Just as adults enjoy watching television sitcoms and movies, children more easily stay focused when the situation is portrayed by the parent in a playful way. Problems with bedtime, eating, upcoming trips, doctor visits, moves, school or day-care changes—can be prepared for by playing out the problem or situation in advance with dolls and stuffed animals as the actors. This does entail some thought and planning to set the stage and play out issues of stress and conflict. A motivated parent could use this creative strategy to deal with problems, provided they have sufficient time during the child's waking hours to do so.

How the child treats his or her dolls and stuffed animals may be a clue as to what the child is experiencing. Continued violent, aggressive play may indicate that the child is being treated too aggressively either by adults or by other children. Parents may find their own expressions of anger, rage, and other feelings mirrored and echoed in their child's doll play. This can alert a parent to the need to change the way they behave with their child. Such play can alert the parent to aggressive or abusive substitute caregiving.

DRESS-UP AND DRAMATIC PLAY

Dress-up and dramatic play stimulate imagination, fantasy, and roll identification. As an adjunct to doll play, and for further dramatic play, it helps to have dress-up clothes and costume materials available. Cast-off shoes, hats, purses, scarves, ribbons and belts, and large squares of cloth delight preschoolers and school-age children. Capes, crowns, and firefighters' hats can stimulate fantasy play and enjoyment. Actively playing out multiple roles rehearses the child for future adult activities, as well as reinforcing much that the child is learning.

Parents should not deny themselves the pleasure of watching these wonderful, spontaneous and unique dramatic productions.

Encouraging and Facilitating Reading

"Once upon a time, there was a family with a little boy and little girl and they were about to move to a new house. . . ." What is the pleasure of storytelling? It may be that the storyteller is creatively expressing something that is particularly meaningful for the child. The story may be personal, from the storyteller's life. It may be a familiar folk tale. Perhaps it holds a specific lesson, or is related to a current problem the child has. It may be funny or fantastic, something both parent and child can enjoy and laugh at together. Or the story may be from a favorite book.

Along with play, storytelling and reading aloud make for many positive childhood memories. It is not unusual for the preschool child to want to hear certain stories over and over again, as one enjoys listening to familiar music.

The storyteller's voice, while telling or reading a tale, needs to have enough variety in inflection and intensity to lend interest to the tale. But, if it is too dramatic, the child loses connection with the story and focuses instead on the adult, becoming preoccupied (or frightened) by the emotions being expressed.

Picture books that illustrate the objects and events in the child's world delight preschoolers. Finding, naming, and describing what he or she sees in the pictures are part of the child's pleasure and encourages the use of language and the building of vocabulary.

Poetry, rhyme, and nonsense sounds also have their place in the enjoyment of language and the positive connection to books. Stories such as "Good Night Moon" have their pleasure in the rhyme as well as the pictures and words. Collections of children's poetry may be enjoyed by preschoolers, especially when the parents also like this kind of reading. Encouraging children to rhyme, and to play with sounds, adds another dimension to the enjoyment of language and, later, to the love of books.

Reading to a young child, or looking at pictures with one, or telling stories that have already been told, enhances the parent-child bond as well as widening a child's language skills, cognitive development, and pleasure in reading. When can this activity take place? Usually, reading or looking at books takes place before naps or during "quiet" times,

A child who enjoys listening to a parent will more likely listen to a teacher.

for example after a midday walk or playtime in the park. At such an "unwinding" time, the child may welcome the quiet stimulation and pleasure of a familiar story or book while sitting close to the parent. Moreover, a child who learns to enjoy listening to a parent's reading is likely to learn how to concentrate when, later, he or she goes to school and needs to be able to listen to teachers.

This kind of relaxed, pleasurable reading is often difficult for working parents to provide. In the few hours after they return from work and before the child is put to bed, they do not have enough time to talk, to reminisce, or to share the pleasure of books. Other activities take priority: baths, meals, clean-up. So the end of a busy day is not the optimum time to enjoy a reading experience. The tired parent usually wants to "hurry up" and "get through the story" and put the child to bed. The child—who feels a need to be with the parent—often becomes disruptive in an attempt to delay bedtime, and thus prolong the pleasure of the parents' presence. The child refuses to get into pajamas, refuses to brush teeth. The exasperated parent exclaims, "All right—it's taking you so long to get ready for bed that there is no time for a story tonight."

But the mother or father who can stay home is not dependent upon these few pressured hours before bedtime. The "at-home" parent can provide a relaxed reading experience at various times during the day, when both parent and child need a quiet time. It follows that the child who has had the daily presence of the parent is more likely to be willing and able to "separate" in the evening, to go to sleep willingly, knowing that mom or dad will be there in the morning to play or to read.

Supervising the Media: Television and Videos

Just as parents are concerned with the quality of a child's diet, they need to be concerned with the quality of the child's visual and auditory stimulation. As early as the toddler years, a child can be captivated by television images. This powerful unpaid baby-sitter competes for time and attention that otherwise might be spent in reading, storytelling, talking, listening, and singing, all of which associate the parent (or caregiver) with pleasure and verbal learning. Adults can all too easily let the child watch television. But when television replaces time spent together, it deprives child and parent of a positive experience so necessary to sustain bonding.

If a child gets most of his or her pleasure from television instead of from interactions with parents, it may be harder for the child to pay attention to adults and (later) to teachers. Unless the parent replaces the passive pleasure television offers with more active stimulation, the child may get in the habit of tuning the parent out. The problem with television, videos, and audio tapes is that the child cannot stop the flow, cannot ask questions, cannot get a personal response. *The child and the media cannot interact*. Moreover, the child has little or no control over the content or pace of the stimulation. The child is denied the natural impulse to question, to elaborate, or to respond with his or her own experiences and feelings. In contrast, when an adult tells a story or reads a book, the child can be a more active listener, can participate in the story, can ask questions and be responsive, can use his or her imagination.

Dr. Sally Ward was the principal speech and language therapist for the Central Manchester Healthcare Trust in England. She tested 1,000 children. She found that constant high decibel levels of background noise from radio and television caused delay in language development. She began her research in 1984 after she detected delayed language development in a growing number of children at her Longstreet Clinic. She devised a test to identify unusual listening behavior as opposed to deafness, and found that babies often ignore human voices, thus depriving themselves of early language learning.

> **Constant high decibel levels of background noise from radio and television cause delay in language development.**

After analyzing and comparing data in a study done six years later, she found that the proportion of youngsters doubly disadvantaged with both listening and talking problems rose from 12 percent to 20 percent. Dr. Ward feels that the constant noise from television, videos, and hi-fi systems was to blame. She found that when parents turn off the television and spend an hour a day communicating and playing with their children without the competition of such extraneous media sounds, children's speech improves as does their ability to listen. Dr. Ward found that there was "Absolutely horrifying noise levels—very loud tellies on constantly—I'm sure it's a good way of keeping kids quiet—three month olds propped in front of videos and older ones with headphones and story tapes."[6] Dr. Ward further found that "[t]elevision has come to dominate and impoverish relationships in the home, particularly between adults and children."[7]

This is not to say that some limited television watching is not stimulating and nurturing. Television does widen children's experiences, and can increase their vocabulary and understanding of the world. But finding age-appropriate television programs may be difficult. The parent also needs to feel comfortable about saying "no," turning off the set, and dealing with the ensuing protests. Warning and preparation may help. And the parent (or other adult) who spends "special time" with the child *immediately* after the television is turned off will be providing an alternative pleasure. (For preschoolers, television should be turned off at least an hour before bedtime, as well as during family mealtimes.)

Parents, absentee or at-home, have a problem establishing television limits and rules. For one thing, adults themselves are susceptible to being addicted to television; they may not realize how much the set is on during the day. For another, they may not realize that the constant intrusive presence of television is negatively overstimulating the child. Even cartoons, which parents tend to assume are benign, may unwittingly scare a child. If parents take time to talk about television shows in the same way other things are reviewed and explained, much of these frightened reactions can be reduced; watching a program with a parent may help a child feel safer even when the content of the program is "scary." But how much control of what a child sees and hears does a parent have when he or she is away all day?

The use of television, videocassettes, and audiotapes in day care and family care centers, and by substitute caregivers at home, is increasing. Typically, child-care facilities now schedule television-watching time over which parents have little control.

Use of television and video cassettes are increasing in day care and family care centers.

Jonathan, age two and a half, told his mother he was "scared" by the videotape he saw at his center. When questioned, the teacher said an older child brought the tape to share: "After all, it was made by Disney especially for children." But so many Disney productions seem filled with frightening events: death of a parent, monster-like characters, protagonists being lost, kidnapped, or involved in danger. Most of the literature upon which Disney stories are based (fairy tales and so on) were written for school-age children, approximately six to twelve years old. It was not designed for toddlers and other preschoolers. In short, there are few tapes or movies that are age-appropriate for preschoolers, whether or not the parent is present.

Sadly, money is made from producing violent action films. Since language skills need not be highly developed to understand acts of aggression, the media tends to produce, increasingly, more programs containing violence both for children and foreign export. In such films, dialogue is often secondary, which obviates the need for much in the way of language and helps those who produce the film to increase their profits. On the other hand, comedy and romantic dramas depend on the subtlety of language to be understood and enjoyed.

Unfortunately, the fearful images a child sees on television and videotapes may reinforce their own anxieties and confirm an underlying concern that the world is unsafe and that he or she is unprotected and vulnerable. Furthermore, children who experience anger and rage see violent acts as a solution for their own stresses. Television seldom models alternative behaviors for dealing with aggression. In fact, adults who watch the local news are more likely to feel that their own community is in danger. Consciously or otherwise, such adults communicate such concerns and fears to their children. Thus, through the medium of television, murder, rape, and tragedy intrude into most homes on a daily basis. This is despite the fact that most of the time such tragedies and trauma do not occur either close to home or even in the same community. Studies have shown that on the average, most prime-time newscasters will report four or five violent events on the evening news. If these events do not occur in their own community, they will "import" such events from some other community, which can be hundreds or even thousands of miles away.[8]

It is certainly understandable that many authorities are questioning the long-range impact on our society of the daily viewing of violence and tragedy—primarily on television. In addition to any action, or lack of it, taken by our leaders, it clearly behooves all parents to take increased responsibility in supervising age-appropriate television and media watching for their children. Both the quality as well as quantity of such external stimulation must be evaluated and controlled to minimize adverse effects of the media.

Teaching Discipline

Most parents want to raise a disciplined child. However, they often fail to see the relationship between their active presence and effort, and the kind of behavior their child ultimately displays. A disciplined child can be defined as one who:

- behaves appropriately for his or her age and stage of development;
- is independently motivated to play, study, and work;
- can recognize various emotions and feelings and begin to form appropriate controls and outlets for those feelings;
- can learn the rules of family, neighborhood, and school, including respect for privacy and property; and
- is able to delay immediate satisfactions and pleasures in favor of longer range satisfactions.

Disciplined behavior must be taught. Children are not born knowing how to behave. And they must be taught it like any other subject—both in and out of school. Good teaching depends on:

- helping a child develop a sense of trust in the adult. A child needs to feel safe and cared for; learning discipline is difficult when he or she feels anger, fear, or disappointment in someone who fails the child by not being present and available. Learning new kinds of behavior or learning self-control is stimulated by secure, loving attachments; the desire to please the caregiver becomes a part of the child's motivation to learn, to grow, and to obey.

- a reasonable expectation that children can learn what caregivers want them to learn. Whether this expectation is or is not reasonable will depend upon the children's ages, abilities, social pressures, and past histories.
- the caregiver clearly communicating to the child what is expected, so that the child understands what the caregiver wants. For most preschoolers, verbal directions and expectations may not be enough. Acting out the desired behavior with dolls and stuffed animals help the child to prepare for and practice what is expected. Preparation for the coming change in routine needs to be discussed. For example, the child needs to hear about the arrival of a new bed, what will happen to the child's crib, and when and how this transition will take place.
- evaluating the child's behavior by telling him or her what he or she did well and what still needs work, just as teachers test children to determine what has been learned and what needs further practice.
- allowing the child to try again. Practicing and rehearsing is essential in all learning.
- the caregiver finding a time and place where less-disciplined behavior and feelings can be expressed. A bedroom or backyard can provide the privacy needed for such things as messing, throwing, spitting, screaming, and making noise.
- once learned or accomplished, disciplined behavior can be acknowledged and recognized. But too lavish a reaction may interfere with the child's pleasure in his or her own accomplishment. Too lavish praise may also create added, hidden pressure.

Teaching disciplined behavior is complex. It takes planning, time, effort and thought.

As all of these requirements indicate, teaching disciplined behavior is a complex matter and requires thought, planning, time, and effort. Yet as we bemoan the fact that children grow up undisciplined, we forget how much adult presence and effort is required to teach appropriate behavior. Inculcating discipline takes time.

Unfortunately, parents who feel guilty about their day-long absence, and perhaps also feel competitive with the caregiver who *has* been with the child all day, may be reluctant to set limits. The parents may unwittingly be seductive and indulgent, not wanting to contaminate the few hours they are able to share with the child before bedtime with issues about disciplined behavior.

If parents are available during most of the day they feel less guilty and more willing to set limits, and to cope with negative emotional responses. They also feel more comfortable in dealing with the child when disciplined behavior is required.

MODELING DISCIPLINE

One important method of teaching disciplined behavior is for the caregiver to model it. But parents need to be there to teach desirable behavior by example. In speaking to a group of parents, the late Bruno Bettleheim, an expert in child raising, mentioned that it seems to take "an infinite number of parental examples of self-control and patience to teach disciplined behavior and to influence the child to internalize positive values."[9]

Some examples of this follow:

- We cannot expect a child to stop hitting others when the primary caregiver continues to hit or spank.
- Parents or other caregivers who use profanity cannot expect the child to develop control of "toilet talk."
- If mother and father do not fasten their seat belts every time, it will be harder for the child to learn to do so. Parents need to obey stop signs, red lights, and parking restrictions if they expect their children to develop a growing respect for society's rules.
- It is hard to teach our children to respond promptly to shifts in the day's activities if the parent or caregiver does not pick them up at preschools, day care, or a friend's house at the expected time.

- We cannot expect children to use appropriate words to express their angry feelings (instead of blows or tantrums) if adults do not model for them how to resolve differences through communication.

  Children need to observe their parents behave in a disciplined manner.

- Parents should understand the consequences if they lie or brag and joke about getting away with breaking a law. This behavior not only sets a bad example but communicates a double message about morality.
- Predictable daily routines around eating, sleeping, and play model the parent's commitment to order and discipline. Parents do not model disciplined behavior when they allow their child to remain hungry, get overtired, or have no time for play.
- If we want children to listen to *us*, it is important that we take time to listen to *them*. It is not always easy to stop what you are doing and focus on your child's communications. If we often respond to our child's signals with "in a minute" or "later," we are modeling nonresponsiveness. Therefore we cannot be surprised when the child will not listen to us, or fails to respond to us.

Parents who are routinely away from home, working or traveling, are not available as active models. Thus the child may be deprived of the chance to see how they behave themselves in a disciplined manner. Several important consequences occur when the parent is not at home:

1. The parent cannot be aware of most of the child's negative behavior.

2. The parent has little control over how the caregiver reacts to various behaviors of the child.

3. Positive behavior may not be taught, or may be taught skimpily.

4. If the discipline imposed by a substitute caregiver is sadistic or punitive—threats, spankings, physical restraints—

the parent may never know unless the child is old enough to report it. Threats used by substitute care-givers have included: calling the police, telling the child a monster will come, the child will be locked or sent away, mom and dad will not come back if the child does not obey.

5. The child, if punished, may not clearly understand why he or she is being punished or how to behave differently.

6. Since daily discipline is usually handled by a substitute caregiver, when working parents get home they may find their child will not behave or listen to them. That is because the child does not consider the working parent as the primary caregiver; therefore he or she feels less of an obligation to pay attention to parental requests. Indeed, the child may respond more appropriately to the substitute caregiver with whom an attachment *has* developed, and to whom he or she must relate most of the day.

Children who do not sense a complete commitment from their working parents often have a harder time responding to the demands of their parents and society, and may be more likely to have problems with the rules and expectations for disciplined behavior. Discipline problems because of absentee parents can be compared to the difficulties faced, for example, by a substitute teacher who arrives to teach a class. He or she finds that the children, who are usually cooperative with their regular teacher, are unruly and undisciplined. These students feel free to act up because they have no relationship with this new teacher.

Encouraging the Development of a Conscience: Moral and Social Values

Children are not born with a conscience. They do not automatically grow up with a sense of honesty, fairness, generosity, or kindness. Rather, these moral and social values are learned at critical times in the child's development.

In their book *High Risk: Children Without a Conscience*, Magid and McKelvey write: "A baby's recognition of his mother's voice and face is designed to enhance the bonding and attachment process. As we have noted, it is through the parent-child attachment that the baby's energy becomes regulated, channeled and transformed into healthy growth. This is the start of the socialization process that provides the growing child with an inner sense of trust and well-being. With socialization the forming of a conscience has begun."[10]

A conscience—which is a set of values, prohibitions, and "rights and wrongs"—has its beginnings in the early bonding and attachment process. If there is consistent nurturing and protection in the preverbal years the child feels loved, respected, and cherished, and learns to trust. In turn, the child will begin to identify with the values and standards of the important adults in his or her life, and imitate and internalize their values. But this process requires *consistent* and responsive caregiving during these first three years of life. As we have said before, when the primary caregivers during this period change frequently, infants and toddlers have difficulty learning to trust and form secure attachments. Because of this, at a later age, the child's ability to introject the values of their adult caregivers can be impaired. Many of these children may have severe social and behavioral problems as adolescents and adults because they lack a developed conscience. As Selma Fraiberg states, "Where there are no human attachments, there can be no conscience. As a consequence, these hollow men and women contribute very largely to the criminal population."[11]

> **Conscience has its beginnings in the early attachment process.**

But if the parent, as the stable and responsive caregiver, has established a positive and secure attachment to the child in the first three years of life, it is more likely that such children, when about five to nine years old, will adopt the values of the parent.

But adopting parental values is not an automatic process, either. Whether the child will adopt such values or not depends not only upon the establishment of the close relationship with the parent in the first three years, but also upon the *continuing* and positive parental presence in the *later* years of childhood. As we shall see, the absence of a parent when the child returns home from school can also create serious obstacles to the development and introjection of moral values.

In comparing the influence of parents and other persons in the development of values, Dr. Penelope Leach had this to say: ". . . the less time children and parents spend together and the fewer thoughts and activities they share, the more powerful secondary influences are likely to be. Growing, changing, developing children cannot be left on ice when parents are not around, so time and space in minds and hearts get filled by other people."[12]

Most parents hope and expect their children to learn and practice traditional values of honesty, candor, and respect for the rights of others. Such moral values are learned over many years of a child's development, but more intensely so between the ages of five and nine. It is during these critical years that most children will experiment with lying, cheating, and

> *Most children will experiment with lying, cheating and stealing.*

stealing. And it is during these same years that they learn the rules they should follow at home, at school, and in their community. It is helpful if compatible rules and values are taught and reinforced both at school and at home.

It has become popular in contemporary America for some parents with delinquent children to place the blame for their children's behavior upon the failure of our educational system and its teachers. We often hear such parents complain: "If the schools did their job instead of coddling students, kids would learn to obey the laws and rules of society." These parents would do well to think about whether or not *their* role as absentee parents may have something to do with their children's antisocial behavior.

In considering absentee working parents and the development of values we wish to see inculcated in our children, I have observed that many recognize the importance of families producing good citizens with positive social values. But parents seem to forget what little input they have during the week as they work away from their children. Concerning these children, Dr. Leach states, "Instead of learning to do as adults *do*, children are expected to do as adults *say*. Discipline that is achieved by the exercise of power can never be as effective as self discipline achieved through influence."[13] (emphasis added). It seems clear then that if parents are absent during so much of the child's waking hours, the primary influence for the transmission of values must come from whatever substitute is caring for the children at the time.

Children need to be taught what is expected of them, and that they are accountable for their behavior. They need to learn to obey society's expectations, rules, and routines. In order to hold children accountable, an adult presence is almost always required. It seems obvious that if parents are absent during the work week, they usually do not know about a child's specific antisocial acts; they cannot even attempt to question the child's behavior or to hold the child accountable. If four-year-old Peter takes a toy car from a friend's house, the absentee parent may never know about the stealing because a substitute caregiver does not report it, either for lack of attention or neglect, or simply that the substitute forgot.

> *In order to hold children accountable, an adult presence is required.*

That is one extreme; at the other, a substitute caregiver may indeed take note of the incident and discipline the child by "branding" him or her a thief. This may have a damaging effect upon Peter's self-concept; or it may unwittingly encourage him to be a more effective and secretive thief. One would hope that a parent, confronted with the incident, would kindly but firmly explain: "I know you like that toy car, but you must remember it belongs to your friend. He also likes the toy, and since it belongs to him, it is important that you return it. If you like, I will go with you."

Peter's story may seem an isolated and unimportant event, but it is precisely such an event that can be used to teach the values of private property and socially acceptable behavior.

Many incidents that occur during the critical school-age years can help children learn to follow the laws of society. Consider eight-year-old Vickie. She says her brother does all the "bad" things at home: "He is the one who ruins everything and should be blamed." Vickie denies her own responsibility completely. Parents who are there are in a position to see to it that Vickie becomes accountable for her *own* mischief. However, they also need to respect her ability to use her imagination to distort and fantasize. Her mom could say: "Your little brother sure gets you into trouble, but you still need to help me clean up the mess *you* made." Or, "I like the stories you make up and it is fun to pretend, but we have to fix the record player that was broken while you were playing with it."

School-age children become quite skillful at lying and conning, and as the child spends more time away from home it is hard even for the "at-home" parent to know where the child is and what the child is doing. But at least the parent who is present when the child comes home from school has a better opportunity to observe, to ask and to listen. In the typical latch-key situation it is almost impossible for the parent to do that.

Nor do absent parents have any idea if what the child tells them is accurate. For example, when the parent asks, "Janey, where did you get that toy?" Janey may lie and say, "My friend Jennifer gave it to me." The fact may be that Janey simply took the toy without paying for it while at the market with her babysitter. If the parent had been with Janey at the market, the theft might never have occurred or she might have become aware later in the car or at home that Janey had taken the toy. Then the parent is in a position to say: "Janey, we will have to go back to the store and either give the toy back, or pay for it. It is against the rules to take something without paying. We will help you find a way to get another toy like this one if you want it badly. But you need to tell us so we can help you learn to obey the rules. Of course, I'll go back to the store with you and help explain to the manager that you took it and are returning it."

The absent parent loses the opportunity to promptly observe and detect such conduct. Moreover, without this confrontation Janey may continue to steal and lie about it without being discovered. Janey may never become account-able for many small acts of lying and stealing during her school-age years, and grow to adulthood burdened by this legacy.

> *The absent parent loses the opportunity to observe, detect and confront antisocial behavior.*

It should not be assumed that evening and weekend parenting has no impact on the child's developing conscience. On the contrary, parents can make practical efforts to teach moral values when they are with their child. Mealtime is another good time to reinforce positive and social values.

Providing Time to Plan Family Activities, Parties, Field Trips, and Preparing the Family Meal

By six o'clock five-year-old Jonathan is too hungry to wait for his mom to come home at 6:30 and fix dinner, so his sitter pops a frozen meal into the microwave. He eats his food while glued to his favorite television program. He holds the plate close to his mouth as he shovels in the food. Jonathan's sister, Nancy, sometimes helps her mother fix dinner, but then takes her plate to her room and eats while on the phone with her friends, or while watching her own television set. Depending on dad's schedule, he may or may not make it home before 8:00 P.M. He, too, may eat a warmed-up dinner alone. This family's meal has become a fragmented casualty of having two working parents.

Arranging family activities takes time. This is true whether we consider planning a vacation, a party, or even planning everyday meals—particularly the evening meal. While families can enjoy the evening meal together even though both parents work all day, it is not easy. We are not talking about the tiny percentage of homes where a hired housekeeper has all day to shop and plan and serve tasty meals. Instead, the average family relies on a family member—often mom—to do the shopping and plan the meals so the family can eat together.

At mealtime the tensions of hunger and fatigue are lessened. The body is rejuvenated. It is a good time for children to be exposed to new words and ideas, to conflicts and solutions, to world and neighborhood events. It is a good time for them to listen and to talk about values and feelings. No wonder that so many successful people fondly recall—and emphasize—the importance of family meals in their childhood years. They tell us how mealtimes provided a window into their parents' lives, and into the outside world. They learned to listen to their brothers and sisters, and to observe and practice table manners. They were involved in a variety of family matters. All of this took place while they were enjoying food and drink.

Ideally, during the usual time that dinner may take, parents can find out a little about the child's day. Without realizing it, children can practice their verbal skills, expand their vocabulary, and feel that someone who cares is listening to them and is interested in them. In reality, most meals for preschoolers last about five minutes as they become squirmy relatively quickly after eating.

But the last 30 or 40 years has seen a decline in the concept of the "family meal." It is sad today to see how many family members grab a plate of food from the kitchen and plop down in front of the television alone (whether or not they are all home at the same time). Children often watch their own programs in another room and eat in isolation from the parent, not even sharing the television experience. If

The family meal has steadily declined in the last 30 or 40 years.

they do watch the same program the focus is on the screen. There is little or no family discussion, except perhaps a battle over what to watch. Thus a great opportunity is lost; family members are deprived of a valuable social and educational experience.

At mealtimes (providing the family does eat together), parents and children may plan to discuss a variety of topics. Children may want to fight over who has the best spoon or the biggest portion, or who is sitting next to whom. However, it is always important to assure that what is presented and discussed is age appropriate. Ideally, such topics may include:

- what happened at work or school;
- plans for future trips, moves, vacations, parties, purchases, and so on;
- evaluations of past events and celebrations;
- weather, and how to prepare for it;
- values such as honesty, loyalty, friendship, generosity, compassion—all of which can be explored via anecdotes;
- reminiscences about family lore and parents' childhood experiences; and
- family problems, stresses, and complaints.

The serious topics should not be discussed in a grim and unpleasant manner. Keeping the talk casual and friendly, even though the subject matter may be serious, is more effective. Plenty of opportunity for humor, giggles, and laughter add to the enjoyment of the mealtime experience. Some silence may also be welcome.

To sum up, it seems obvious that the institution of the family meal offers all sorts of opportunities for positive and joyful interaction between parents and children, even if more and more such meals may be occurring in restaurants. Sadly, however, sharing meals, as a family at home, appears to be increasingly neglected all week long—and even on Sundays!

The Parental Role in Teaching Sexual Information

When and how we communicate sexual information with the preschooler is extremely important. Luckily, all this information is not imparted at one time. The story unfolds over the years, demystifying this loaded area as the child expresses interest and is able to comprehend.

Most parents wish to control the sexual information given to their child.

Questions may be asked at any time of the day by the child. How they are answered may influence the child's attitudes dealing with this important subject for years to come.

Adults may show embarrassment, anger, shock, pleasure, or interest in communicating sexual information when questioned. Children can receive a subtle message that "we don't talk about this subject" or the information can be frightening, inaccurate, or overwhelming. On the other hand, the message can be satisfying and interesting and lead to further discussion dealing with sexual matters.

Too much information on this subject too soon may turn off, frighten, or overwhelm the child. Too little explanation and information may leave the child curious and unsatisfied. Initially it is the parents who are usually involved in the teaching of sexual information to their young child. Later, teachers, books, and films may add to this information base.

Sexual education includes a large variety of facts, attitudes, and experiences, such as:

- anatomical concepts and biological differences between male and female;
- where babies come from and how they are born;
- expected bodily changes during adolescence;
- development of erotic feelings and the time and place for expressions; and
- development of positive attitudes toward one's own and the opposite sex.

A three year old may question "Where did I come from?" or "How did you get me?" Some children may never verbalize directly but instead are insatiably curious (like Kipling's "The Elephant Child"). Some may obsessively ask "why," never really asking the real question they want answered.

It is easy to see that teaching this complicated subject may be difficult even for motivated parents who want to communicate effectively! However, what can also be distressing and frustrating is that parents have no idea how substitute caregivers deal with subjects such as birth, anatomy, menstruation, masturbation, and sexual identity when these matters arise during the parents' working day. It is also true that most parents feel that they want to know or be in control of how these subjects (loaded as they are) are responded to.

The Importance of Being There!

Even motivated, loving parents will fail to address some aspects of their child's development optimally. Some moms or dads may enjoy and involve themselves in the child's play experiences more than others. Some parents will be more vigilant in teaching disciplined behavior. Others are concerned with health, safety, and protection. All come to the role of caregiver with their own psychological strengths and deficits. But most want to communicate profound feelings of love and caring to their children.

As I meet with parents, I sometimes feel I am remiss in talking so much about what our children "need" from the pre-verbal through the adolescent periods, and what negative results can occur if these needs are ignored. But let us not forget the positive benefits that parents receive in return, in spite of the hard work and frustrations. For one thing, they have the opportunity to participate, hour by hour and day by day, in thousands of interactions with their children: playing peek-a-boo, singing, comforting, rocking, feeding, painting, bicycling, skating, ball throwing, talking, explaining, teaching, and yes—at times—scolding. Additionally, they are present to mutually enjoy with their child many developmental "firsts." They are there when the first steps are taken, the first words echoed or spoken, the first use of the potty, the first ball caught, when a painting or drawing begins to show a creative leap, or when conversations begin to yield mature and sometimes surprising concepts, or their humor stimulates laughter.

In other words, both mothers and fathers have the chance, during the few years their children are "growing up," to truly know, enjoy, and experience the child in most aspects of his or her life. A parent reported to me his euphoria after his son, an uninspired player, caught a fly ball in a little league game. His pleasure was boundless at that moment. Many such opportunities are *forever* lost if mom and dad are both away from home all day, every weekday. Conversely, every moment that a parent can provide a meaningful presence can bring lifetime rewards, pleasures, and memories for the family. Isn't this what is meant by the joys of parenthood?

But for any mother or father, the joys of parenting are hard to achieve without the presence of a spouse or reliable support system. Caring for a child at any age in a loving and responsive way demands vigilance, effort, energy, and an abiding, cheerful enthusiasm. For a woman, this maternal

The joys of parenting are hard to achieve without a spouse.

energy may be instinctive, a natural force that helps species survive. Some of this strength may arise from having received in her past loving care from her own parents. But a major source of this energy comes from the support, understanding, and affection a mother feels from her mate. An infant does not need to be cared for by more than one parent. But a mom (or a dad) needs a spouse to "be there"—to infuse the caregiving parent with love, kindness, and an extra pair of hands. These hands, at times, can help with pushing a vacuum, shopping, picking up a video, walking a crying child, or hugging the stressed-out partner.

Dr. Karen Schachere, in an article dealing with working mothers, states that, "[a] full time working mother's ability to respond contingently and sensitively to her infant may require a husband who not only supports her maternal caregiving, but participates willingly in basic household tasks."[14] This is also true for the stay-at-home mother.

A spouse can be a link to the outside world, nurturing the stay-at-home parent with a glimpse into his or her working day, reporting on gossip, tragedies, or humor. It is also evident that older children benefit greatly by receiving the love, attention, and stimulation from another person with whom he or she forms an attachment.

The differences in behavior, temperament, and physical attributes that two people can provide can greatly enrich the life of a child. All of the child's emotional eggs are not in one basket. The child has the opportunity to depend upon and rely upon both parents or another primary attachment figure for protection, support, comfort, and fun. The fear of abandonment by a single parent is reduced when two or more attachment figures are involved with the child.

WHAT TIMMY WANTS FROM A DAD

Timmy, in Chapter 1, told us what he needs from a mom. If he could express what he would want from a dad or other partner, he might say:

I want my dad to be there for my mom to comfort and soothe her in labor, to rejoice with her at my birth, and to understand her discomforts and her pains while she adjusts to motherhood.

I want a dad to hold me when I need a strong pair of arms, a new rhythm of walking when my mom is fading.

I want a dad to play with different words, different jokes, different games, different songs.

I want a dad to teach me to use my body and mind to give me a feeling of competence to compete and feel the pride of new skills.

I want a dad to bring me the outside world, a dad who has exciting tales to share, who obeys laws and rules and is responsible, and is a dad I can respect.

I want a dad who will carry me when my legs give out, who will stop me when I lose control, and who does not frighten me by his own strength and power.

I want a dad from whom I can learn how to love a woman [if I'm a boy] or [if I were a girl] experience the trust and pleasure of love from a man.

A dad could represent any committed person who provides consistent support for the child and his or her primary caregiver.

7

Solutions:
How to Provide Continuity of Quality Care

I t is understandable if some working parents, after reading the preceding chapters, feel upset, uneasy, guilty, or angry. This may be true especially for parents whose young children have already experienced separations and losses traceable to frequent changes of caregivers. But these parents can take comfort in recognizing past problems and providing a more secure and predictable future environment. Moreover, children have a surprising amount of resilience. They may be able to overcome early attachment deficits through reparative relationships, both with parents and other adults; or even, if indicated, via psychotherapy. Bowlby described these hopeful possibilities in his comments about future emotional prospects of infants who were deprived of the opportunity to form attachments in the first six months of life. He felt that they would suffer less emotional damage—and that the effects of such damage would be far less— if these infants received timely positive nurturing after the first six months.[1] This chapter is addressed to two categories of parents:

- expectant parents and new parents who *are* financially able to provide continuity of care for their preverbal children themselves by acting as primary caregivers; and
- parents of infants and toddlers who have made the decision that they will work (either part- or full-time) and provide substitute child care.

Most parents of infants and toddlers face the following conflicts:

- job commitments versus home obligations and chores;
- acquisition of material possessions and career development versus time spent at home with their young children;
- earning the money to buy and pay for a home, versus renting an apartment; and
- a lifestyle that includes vacations and new cars *now* versus postponing these pleasures to a later time.

As we consider the following suggested solutions to these conflicting options, let us keep in mind two main facts that apply to substitute care for infants and toddlers. First, when the primary caregivers are *not* the parents, frequent changes of substitute caregivers—sometimes as often as every few months—are the rule and not the exception. And second, these changes increasingly cause emotional damage to the *young* child.

Substitute caregivers change as often as every few months.

Before parents decide either to employ substitute caregivers or to render care themselves, or to use a combination of both methods, it is well to keep in mind the following considerations:

1. the availability and extent of the family's financial resources;

2. how many hours per day and per week substitute care will be needed;

3. availability of relatives, friends, and neighbors to help with caring for the child; and

4. flexibility of parental job/career commitments. Often, a father's job commitment may allow him to be home for many more hours than the mother's. He can then act as primary caregiver during this time.

With these considerations in mind, we will now consider practical methods by which young children can be given continuity of quality and nurturing care. First, let us look at how such care may be provided by parents and, second, by nonparental substitutes.

Practical Methods by Which Parents Can Provide Primary Care

ARE ASSETS AVAILABLE TO THE PARENTS?

Parents often forget that they have assets that, if they are willing to use them, will allow a parent to stay home with the young children (for the limited period we have discussed). These assets can include: savings accounts, stocks and bonds, and trusts, or other similar assets whose funds can be dipped into if good reasons can be demonstrated to the trustees.

Parents are often unwilling to use assets for child care, even when they are available.

Some parents may be reluctant to "invade" such savings or trusts for the purpose of child care. However, the goal of this book is to persuade such parents of the need to be present in those early years, even though they may have to deplete a financial nest egg. Of course this involves a question of priorities. Which is more important: preservation of the assets for some later pressing need, or using the assets to allow a parent to stay home *now* and more effectively bond with the infant?

This is not an easy decision. Parents may well agonize over the pros and cons of using up funds they would prefer to save for the proverbial rainy day. Nor is their decision made any easier by the fact that there will undoubtedly be advice and pressure from friends, relatives, and others to allow the assets to remain untouched and available for some future need. And it may be hard for parents to appreciate the importance of their child's early months and of avoiding the risks of caregiver roulette (as explained in Chapter 4).

BORROWING MONEY TO STAY HOME
FOR ONE OR TWO YEARS

No one likes to borrow money. But almost all of us do it for a variety of reasons: to buy a car, to buy a home, to replace major appliances, to pay college tuition, and so on. On the assumption that the well-being of your child is at least as important—if not more so—than these reasons why not consider taking out a loan to supplement family finances and allow you, as parent, to supply what your child needs?

In our credit-oriented culture, there are many ways parents can borrow money. Following are a few.

- *Bank or Credit Union Loans.* These are usually installment loans made when the lender is reasonably sure that the parent involved has sufficient income (or capital) to repay the loan. Banks are eager to make these loans; almost every bank advertises their availability. On the theory that our children are as important as cars and refrigerators, why not take out an installment loan so that a parent can remain home for two years? Or, if two years is not feasible, how about one year? Every month that continuity of care can be provided for an infant and toddler is important.

  In addition to the orthodox bank loan, many employees have the right to borrow money from credit unions affiliated with their employers. Such loans are granted upon the same terms as bank loans, except that employees who are depositors in these credit unions are preferred customers, and thus usually accorded some "priority." In the course of my research, I have talked to several bankers; most are receptive to the idea of making an installment loan for the admittedly unusual purpose of allowing a parent to stay home to take care of the child; they thought this was an excellent idea. Bankers will not need much convincing since they are primarily interested in one thing: will the loan be repaid?

- *Home Equity Loans.* If parents-to-be own a home, they can utilize the equity that many homeowners have already accumulated. In the 1990s, banks throughout the United States are eager to lend money with the family home as security. I have discussed with several the idea of a family making a home equity loan for the purpose of allowing a parent "at-home time" with his or her child. Each banker was enthusiastically positive. Remember: $25,000 or more can go a long way toward providing essential "at-home time" for a parent.

- *Loans (or "Grants") from Grandparents and Other Relatives.* Grandparents, great-grandparents, and other involved relatives who themselves stayed home with their young children may be excellent sources for borrowing. It is surprising how many of the older generation seem sympathetic to the idea that a parent should stay home and care for his or her infant and toddler. Indeed, close relatives might be expected to want the new arrival to have the best possible emotional and intellectual head start.

  Many such relatives traditionally would plan to provide college or other funds for the child. Or, they may plan to leave the child money in their will. It may be hard at first to persuade relatives of the overriding importance of consistent quality care so early in the child's life. But such persuasion can succeed with the use of one or more personalized approaches. First, the relative can be told by the expectant mother or father just how critical the first few years of life are. The importance of a parental presence, as well as some of the problems associated with substitute care, can be discussed. Literature on the subject can be presented. Hopefully, this information, along with parental enthusiasm, will be sufficient motivation to convince a relative to make the loan.

While researching this book, in discussions with families, I found that the most likely source of funds would be grandparents. If asked for a loan rather than a gift, grandparents

Grandparents may be a source of funds.

may be surprisingly willing to comply, especially if they provided primary care for their own children. They may be delighted to hear that the money they lend will allow their grandchild to have a secure beginning and a head start in life.

SAVE MONEY BEFORE THE CHILD IS BORN

This approach requires advance planning and may be a problem if pregnancy is accidental. But why can't parents who plan to have a child start saving before the baby arrives or is conceived? We save for homes, vacations, and cars. We save for future college tuition. Would it not make more sense to put aside some money early in a child's life to help provide a solid emotional foundation? Without such an emotional underpinning, the probability of the child reaching his or her educational potential is seriously in question. As I pointed out earlier, preparing a child to make the most of his or her education starts in the preverbal years, when the child builds (or fails to build) the foundation of trust in caregivers. This later transfers to teachers and other relationships. Only if the child succeeds in building such trust will success in life be a realistic expectation. It seems eminently reasonable to spend money where it will count most—in the child's earliest years.

It is ironic that many parents and family members in the United States, aided and abetted by insurance company advertising, observe the tradition of starting a "college fund"

Money put away for college is of little use to a young adult with a poor attachment history.

for their child—often long before he or she is born. All of us should of course applaud any effort to improve the educational prospects of our children! But, I submit that this kind of financial contribution is sadly misguided, and misplaced in time. "College money" is of little use to a young adult whose early attachment history was chaotic, who had difficulty relating to teachers, and who became a school dropout during adolescence.

Even as I make this suggestion, I realize I am bucking powerful opposition. I refer not only to the financial industry but also to literally centuries of tradition that enshrine the almost holy value of a college education. There is no doubt that to proud new parents, the gift of a tasseled and beribboned "college insurance policy" for the new arrival has far more appeal than the same amount of money given to mom and dad so that at least one parent can defer a return to work and stay home to provide emotional security to the infant. But if our guiding principal is "what is best for baby," the answer seems clear!

CUT BACK ON EXPENDITURES

We all know how seductive it is to raise our standard of living and enjoy an upscale lifestyle. Difficult though it may seem, parents might consider deferring, for the limited period of a few years, such large expenditures as buying a home, or a new car, or an expensive vacation. It is hard not to "keep up with the Joneses" but the trade-off may be well worth it, even though it may take some years to see the result.

Bill and Joan both worked in middle management positions in a large insurance company. At about the time Joan became pregnant with their first child, Bill received a promotion and a substantial salary increase. Their other friends had all moved to an upper-income suburban community and they also felt the social pressure to move to an upscale neighborhood, away from their modest apartment.

However, Joan was looking forward to full-time parenthood. Her own mother supported this decision, as well as her husband. Fortunately, Joan and Bill were not in conflict over this issue as many middle-class couples are today. Often, many of these young people are eager to climb the social

> ladder to a more expensive lifestyle, one their own
> parents may have enjoyed. But, to maintain such a
> lifestyle ordinarily requires dual incomes. Bill and
> Joan made the hard choice. They resolved, at least
> for the time being, to stay in their modest apart-
> ment so Joan could remain home and care for the
> expected child.

There are many "Bills and Joans" who feel, instinctively, that a parental presence is important to children. But most of these couples lack the support and encouragement needed to follow their natural maternal and paternal impulses. Moreover, many parents do not seem to realize that by having one spouse stay at home, the money they would *not* have to pay for substitute care would take up some of this financial slack. Transportation costs to and from work would be eliminated. So would the expense of work clothes, restaurant bills, and other job-related charges.

Whether you are a single parent with limited resources, a two-parent family who is just "making it" from paycheck to paycheck, or a family with a substantial income, the wages that would otherwise be paid to a substitute can be used to cover other expenses so that one parent can stay home. Each additional month that finances allow a parent to provide nurturing primary care is of enormous value to the infant or toddler.

DELAY THE RETURN TO WORK AS LONG AS POSSIBLE

Every additional month that mother (or father) is able to spend building a bond with the child is all to the good. Six months are better than three months; one year is preferable to six months; 18 months far more beneficial to your child than 12 months. So take as much time off from work as possible. Many mothers return to work only to find child-care arrangements so complicated and anxiety provoking that after a few months of work they return to full-time parenting.

WORKING AT HOME

As personal computers and computer networking are utilized more and more in business and industry, some parents may find it possible to work at home. There are many kinds of work that can be carried on from home, whether you are computerized or not: telephone sales, counseling, tutoring, writing, and child care. Motivated parents can find a host of publications that discuss possibilities for home employment, on either a permanent or sporadic basis.

Maxine worked as a bookkeeper and was permitted to take office documents to work on at home. Much of her work was done when her toddler was napping. Maxine also was able to keep an eye on the quality of care provided by the baby-sitter who she hired to help her look after the toddler while she was at the office or while she worked at home.

WORKING PART-TIME

If family finances permit, part-time work will allow a parent to spend more time with the infant and toddler. If, for example, a mother or father is able to work two or three days a week instead of five, or four hours a day instead of eight or ten, the result can be a stronger parent-infant bond, and the consequences of caregiver roulette less damaging. Many professionals or consultants in private practice are able to control their hours at work. They can be the primary caregivers during most of the child's waking hours. Then, when the child sleeps, they can work in their professional capacity.

> *Some parents can control their hours of work.*

Some organizations allow job sharing and flexible hours. Artists, architects, and other craft workers can work in a home/studio environment that does not demand 40 hours plus away from the baby or toddler. Secretaries, medical transcribers, or bookkeeper/accountants may also opt for part-time work.

If the parent returns to part-time work (as opposed to full-time), substitute care should be less difficult to find and to afford. Also, the inevitable changes in such substitute care will be far less stressful to the infant. Here is an example:

After her daughter Laura was born, Jennifer returned to her college teaching job. She lectured to her classes three afternoons a week and hired a young mother to care for Laura during those times. Unfortunately, the substitute caregiver and her husband developed personal problems, and she was unable to continue caring for Laura. But since Jennifer still functioned as the primary caregiver, being away from home only 12 hours or so a week, the bond between Jennifer and Laura remained secure despite the departure of the substitute.

WORK AT PLACE OF EMPLOYMENT
WHERE "JOB SITE" DAY CARE IS AVAILABLE

A small but growing number of employers provide day care at the job site. They realize that this arrangement relieves parental concern, cuts down absenteeism, and increases productivity. More employers will make such provisions in the future. Parents fortunate enough to work in such companies are able to visit with their children during the working day and reinforce the sense of physical contact so comforting to the infant and toddler. And, while such larger, industrial day care centers may have high personnel turnover, the opportunity for a more frequent parental presence is a plus that is most beneficial to the child.

PUT YOUR JOB OR CAREER ON HOLD
FOR ONE OR TWO YEARS

While this method requires advance planning, it *can* be done *if* a parent-to-be is able and willing to try it. We plan years in advance for many careers: engineering, psychology, law, medicine, nursing, and so on. Then we study for many years to attain our goal. Once we have graduated, or obtained a license, or passed a bar examination, or qualified for an official degree, it is more feasible to take time off, since we have already obtained the necessary vocational credentials. Then it is possible to return to work when it is more advantageous for the family.

Knowing that one day they will have children, one or both parents-to-be might plan for a career that will accommodate such a one- or two-year hiatus for parenthood after attaining the goals discussed. Employers may not warmly embrace this concept, but your infant's needs may be more important in these critical early years.

For example, most professionals *could* leave their profession temporarily (or work part-time, or work at home) to provide two years of continuity of parental care. Then the parent could reenter the profession. If the firm cannot or will not rehire the parent, it should be possible to find another job in the same field.

WORKING THE TANDEM SHIFT METHOD
UTILIZING BOTH PARENTS

Later in this chapter the "tandem shift" method will be described in connection with substitute care. It refers to an arrangement in which a single parent teams up with another single parent, with each caring for the children of both while the other is at work. (This arrangement is possible only when both persons work different shifts.)

The same option is available to parents in a nuclear family. For example, father may work the 7:00 A.M. to 3:00 P.M. shift; when he gets home he takes over child care while mother goes to work on a swing shift or night shift. There are many jobs where this arrangement is feasible: hospitals, telephone companies, catalogue sales companies, and gas and electric utilities are just some workplaces that employ shifts around the clock. Often, fathers who are writers, musicians, actors, and lecturers can adjust their work hours so they can be available for child care when mother is involved in a 9-to-5 job. But as with most of the methods we have outlined, this one requires effort and adjustment. Determined parents can make it work, particularly when they realize that it will not last forever.

PARENTS WHO HAVE RETURNED TO WORK CAN TAKE TIME OFF (LUCK AND FINANCES PERMITTING)

Sometimes fortuitous financial events occur. One may get a big raise, receive an inheritance, even win the lottery! Simply because a parent works does not irrevocably exclude the possibility of being able to return to full-time parenting *when finances change.* If finances do permit, a working parent could consider returning to the role of primary caregiver, especially if continuity from substitutes has been hard to arrange. During my research I found that most parents seldom think of this option. Perhaps they should!

Nonparental Substitute Caregivers

THE "STANDARD" NANNY CAREGIVER

Understandably, many parents are forced to return to work and make child-care arrangements. When full-time substitute care is required, a traditional solution for the affluent new parent is to hire a caregiver/nanny to care for the infant at the child's home. It is vital that parents find a cheerful, intelligent and loving caregiver who, one hopes, will make a long-term commitment, ideally for two years.

Here are several suggestions parents can use to avoid frequent changes among full-time caregivers during their child's infancy and toddlerhood:

- *Pay more than the "going rate" in your community.* Keeping in mind the fact that zookeepers generally earn more per hour than people who care for children, offer your child's prospective caregiver an hourly rate that is more than the minimum or the average rate in your community. It is amazing how many professional parents pay a minimum wage to the caregivers of their children. Few of these parents would consider paying a minimum wage to their own office employees. And, when deciding what car to buy or what home to live in, they usually do not settle for the least expensive car or home. If a parent can at least pay more than the going rate for child care, the chances are that continuity on the job will be more likely to be provided. The goal would be to lessen the possibility of your new caregiver looking for a better-paying job. Of course, this suggestion assumes that parents can afford such a "premium" arrangement. In addition, to insure increased motivation to remain on the job, it may help to provide extra benefits such as health insurance, the use of a car, more comfortable living quarters, and so on.

- *Whatever you intend to pay, structure the payment schedule to include a lump sum "bonus" amount at the end of the agreed upon period.* Let us assume you enter into a simple written agreement with the new nanny in which you offer him or her, say, a total of $800 per month for the first year and $900 for the second year (it is good employer psychology to include a raise for year two). Your agreement with the nanny could state that at the end of one year he or she will receive a bonus of $1,000 and an additional

A bonus may help provide continuity.

$1,000 bonus at the end of the second year. This provides an obvious financial incentive for the nanny to stay for the minimum two years.

As difficult as it is to find a nanny who will stay for an extended period, it is often more difficult to find one who is *otherwise* acceptable. After all, a nanny's agreement to stay for two years is irrelevant if he or she lacks the requisite qualifications or has trouble getting along with the family. For example, does he or she have the intelligence to give proper care? Is he or she sufficiently responsible to act properly in emergencies and to protect the infant? Is he or she able to read well, enough to follow simple written instructions and to understand and communicate to the parents issues concerning the infant or toddler? The baby's well being may depend on the caregiver reporting symptoms, following directions in administering medications, telephoning for help and so on. Can she safely use the appliances in the house? Is he or she cheerful and loving and responsive to the children under his or her care?

Caregivers with a different primary language and culture may unwittingly impede the development of the child's feeling of identity with its parents and its culture. The 1994 article in *Zero to Three* by Chang and Pulido, quoting J. Ronald Lally, states: "Children between birth and two years of age are in the midst of forming the core of their identity. They are just beginning to acquire preferences and beliefs. The development of this identity occurs in large part by incorporating the views held by the adults who care for them. If the views of those adults are negative and inconsistent with the values of the family and community, the impact on a child's sense of identity could be devastating."[2]

Therefore, it is essential that the parent be assured that the values and attitudes of the substitute are basically in agreement with those of the parent. This can include areas as diverse as attitudes about discipline, methods of feeding, toilet training, and masturbation. Clearly, employment of such cross-cultural substitutes can present real concerns that should not be swept under the rug.

ADDITIONAL CONSIDERATIONS
IN THE SELECTION OF NANNIES

More important than the language and cultural background of the proposed caregiver are other complex personality factors. Parents need to make their own investigation of applicants rather than unduly depend upon screening agencies or personal letters of recommendation. Before any hiring decision is made, one or both of the parents should actually speak to the nanny's former employers—either personally or by telephone. An applicant's failure or refusal to supply names and telephone numbers of several previous employers raises a warning flag. Even if the experience were in a foreign country, if previous employers out of the United States had the funds to employ a nanny, they will usually have a telephone. Another hurdle may be to find an interpreter to speak to the previous employer, if he or she does not speak English. If such telephone numbers are unavailable, and no other references are provided, great caution should be exercised in hiring the applicant.

EMPLOYMENT OF AU PAIRS FROM FOREIGN COUNTRIES

Au pairs are usually young female caregivers from foreign countries who "live in" and care for children, usually for one year. Even when reputable international employment agencies are involved, the screening can be slipshod and misleading. A 1994 *Time* magazine feature, "Looking for Mary Poppins," revealed disturbing information for any parent considering hiring an au pair. The article suggested that the agencies were at fault for "sloppy screening procedures and poor follow-through when troubles arise." Among the cautionary stories connected with au pairs, the article described a Dutch girl who was charged in a Virginia Court in 1994 with shaking to death an eight-week-old infant.[3] The article also described a study reported in the *Cleveland Plain Dealer* that documented "some 300 cases of trouble in au pair placement."

This is not to say that au pair employment is beyond consideration. On the contrary, the *Time* article also pointed out that many families had good experiences with au pair help. However, agencies responsible for bringing au pairs from foreign countries were faulted for failing to check references, and for taking little or no action when trouble was reported. Many of the au pairs in the article did not even remain for the prescribed one-year period. This leads to another good reason not to employ an au pair: it is far better to employ a domestic caregiver for the entire two-year period in order to avoid emotional damage to infants and toddlers when the au pair leaves.

How To Screen a Prospective Caregiver

Whether parents make the decision to hire any substitute—an au pair or someone else—the two most important areas of inquiry, aside from the applicant's willingness to remain during the period of infancy and toddlerhood, are first, the physical health of the applicant, and second, his or her emotional stability and capacity to nurture your child. Remember: this caregiver will be in total charge of your helpless, dependent, and uncommunicative infant or toddler. Literally, while you are at work the life of the child will be in the hands of this person.

Now let us face perhaps the most difficult aspect of employing a nanny: what questions should you ask? And how do you go about making that final decision: to employ or not to employ a person who is going to care for your infant or toddler. It is one of the most important decisions you will make in dealing with your young child.

DETERMINING THE APPLICANT'S PHYSICAL CONDITION

Steps should be taken to verify that the applicant has no communicable disease, nor any illness that might suddenly disable or incapacitate the applicant. For example, an applicant with hepatitis, tuberculosis, AIDS, or other communicable diseases should be avoided. Not only would certain of these illnesses increase the odds that the prospective caregiver would, over the next few months or years, become sick, but that their infections may spread to the child and other healthy members of the family, causing further disruption and stress. Insofar as older or less healthy applicants are concerned, parents should simply use their best judgment to avoid undue risks and yet not eliminate potentially reliable and otherwise qualified caregivers.

In view of the importance of health considerations, I suggest that a parent require a physical exam of the applicant, select a physician, and pay for the examination. The physician should be told of areas of concern that should be checked, and a written release must be obtained from the applicant so that the physician is free to communicate the results directly to the parents.

An example of a significant physical disability was involved with our "Timmy" from Chapter 1. You will recall that Betty, one of his caregivers, suddenly had to leave, causing Timmy great distress. The reason for Betty's departure was a flare-up of longstanding rheumatoid arthritis. She could neither lift, carry, or properly handle the infant. Had Timmy's mother inquired about Betty's physical problems she might not have hired her in the first place.

DETERMINING THE APPLICANT'S SUITABILITY FOR CAREGIVING

By far the most difficult consideration in the screening process is the determination of the applicant's emotional stability and nurturing capacity. Certain items of personal history and background need to be examined. With as much diplomacy, tact, and sensitivity as possible, the questions that follow should be considered. I realize that many of these questions cover delicate areas and that a parent will not be able easily to obtain all of the necessary information. Parents may feel that some of these questions are too intrusive, and they may be embarrassed or too anxious to ask them. But, in

Personal questions are essential in selection of a caregiver.

order to protect infants and young children, it is important to try to get as much information as possible. Hiring a full-time nanny is a complicated business. When a parent is away from home 40 or more hours a week, there is little time or opportunity to supervise and observe what really goes on. And your young child cannot tell you!

1. *Marital status: is the applicant married, divorced, widowed; or never married?* How an applicant responds to this question may pose an interesting dilemma. For example, let us assume that the applicant states that he or she is happily married. Paradoxically, such an applicant may prove to be quite satisfactory and reliable as a day worker, but not as a live-in. For if the nanny is required to be away from his or her spouse all week long, it may not auger well for a long-term caregiving commitment. On the other hand, someone who is single may prefer to live in, and be more willing to commit to your family. Also, it may not be wise to hire someone who has recently gone through the emotional distress that can accompany widowhood or divorce.

   If there is no spouse it is important to know if the caregiver expects to date and otherwise carry on a normal social life. If he or she is to live in, some inquiry should be made as to whether he or she would be available evenings during the week.

2. *If the caregiver has children, what are their ages?* If the caregiver has young children he or she may feel guilty over leaving them to care for someone else's children. If they are ill, he or she would naturally be reluctant to leave them and there may be an absentee problem. In addition, his or her resentment—if any—might impact his or her ability to be nurturing and compassionate to *your* children. He or she also may be more likely to leave the job. Remember Agnes, one of Timmy's caregivers in Chapter 1, whose own child needed surgery and required her full-time attention. With these factors in mind, it might be wiser to consider a caregiver with

older or grown children who are already out of the house, or at least relatively independent.

3. *Who cared for his or her children when they were young?* If the caregiver stayed home and took care of his or her own children from the time they were born until they became verbal, it may show dedication to the job of parenthood as well as be an indication that he or she knows all the aspects of child care—what to do and how to do it. If the applicant has never had children, when or where has he or she learned the skills of caring for a young child? This would be another area of inquiry. Has he or she had experience taking care of infants and toddlers in the past? Has this experience been in private homes?

4. *How was the applicant treated by his or her own mother and father?* If the applicant was loved and cared for well by his or her own parents, he or she is more likely to be a nurturing and compassionate caregiver to your child. If he or she was mistreated and abused—emotionally, physically or sexually—there is a much higher probability that he or she may not be nurturing and loving with your child. As pointed out previously, many of us reenact events of the past when we become parents or caregivers.

5. *What was the most distressful period in the applicant's childhood?* A question like this might be truthfully answered, but might also bring out the fact that he or she really had no significant period of unhappiness—perhaps only minor stresses such as problems in schools with certain teachers or being "picked on" by older siblings. However, if he or she reports physical or sexual abuse by a relative or neighbor, or that his or her parents were overly strict and punitive, you may be concerned about the quality of caregiving because of a likelihood he or she will repeat the script of his or her childhood. We know, statistically, that child molesters often were themselves abused when they were children.

6. *Has the applicant ever suffered from bouts of depression or other serious mental illness?* This is a "loaded area." It is difficult to ask these personal questions and just as difficult to get accurate answers. But even though you may not get accurate information, an attempt should be made anyway. Also, when checking with previous employers, it is simple to raise this and other questions. For example, questioning may show that the applicant was at times moody and irritable, withdrawn or angry. The parent is safe in assuming that such mood swings and attitudes are likely to be repeated.

   While most people who undergo therapy are able to surmount such problems, for some patients depression can be a recurring phenomenon. It may be advisable to avoid such an applicant. After all, the objective is to have continuity of positive caregiving for the first two years. It is not logical to employ someone who is potentially subject to recurrent mental illness because such an illness may cause a break in the continuity of care for your child. Additionally, the applicant may not be sufficiently responsive, warm, and comforting to your young child when under the emotional stress of depression or other mental illness.

7. *Who cared for the applicant when he or she was an infant and toddler?* Earlier chapters (particularly Chapter 4) explain some of the problems that may arise when infants and toddlers are exposed to multiple caregivers. Although many persons cannot recall much of what occurred during their first two years of life, it is certainly worth asking about that time. Many *do* know, for example, that their mother stayed home and took care of them. This is a positive piece of information that may indicate the foundation of the kind of person you would want to care for your child. On the other hand, if the applicant was frequently shuttled between relatives from earliest infancy, a warning flag should go up. Such

a caregiver may not be able to make a real commitment to your child or be consistently caring.

8. *During the applicant's lifetime, who treated him or her the best and who the worst?* Again, answers to questions like these may provide insight about good and bad experiences to which the caregiver was exposed that may impact his or her ability to be a caregiver for your child. If he or she had many happy experiences and few traumatic ones, this can be a positive sign that he or she will be a cheerful, joyful caregiver. He or she may also be someone who may be a positive addition to your family and one who will contribute a sense of well being to all.

9. *Have there been any past problems with drugs or alcohol?* There are thousands—perhaps millions—of recovering alcoholics who have gone through treatment. If, for example, the applicant admits he or she has had problems with alcohol but "has not had a drink in five years," the parents will have to weigh this against other factors and other applicants. It is well know that alcoholics have great difficulty in giving up drinking, and a large percentage slip back into the use of alcohol. On the other hand, you may have reasons to feel that the applicant is sincere, honest, and worth considering.

10. *What medications does the applicant take regularly?* Certain medications make people sleepy, less responsive, or irritable and edgy. For example, diet pills can cause irritability in some persons who take them. Those who take pills for high blood pressure sometimes say they feel drowsy or lethargic—not exactly desirable qualities if you expect the caregiver to follow an active one year old around and keep the child safe from harm. It may be easier to ask what medications the applicant is regularly taking, and then question about what illness or condition requires the medication.

11. *How would the applicant handle certain issues with your child, such as throwing food, refusing to take naps, thumb sucking, masturbation, use of a pacifier, or head banging?* Admittedly, these are not simple problems to handle even for the most conscientious parent. But it is important to find out if the prospective caregiver typically would take punitive or disciplinary measures if, for example, an 18 month old refused to take his or her nap. On the other hand, a sophisticated applicant may say "Each parent handles these matters differently and I would be guided by how you would like me to deal with them so we can provide consistency of care." Parents must make their own decision as to whether or not the substitute will follow such directives. When parents work a full day, supervision of caregiving is difficult. But, as T. Berry Brazelton suggests, "Go home at unannounced times during the day to check up on what's happening. Always have a reason so the caregiver won't feel she's being watched. It is critical that you know what kind of care your baby is getting."[4] There may be a vast difference in what is expressed by any caregiver verbally involving childcare practices and what actually takes place.

Alternative Arrangements for Substitute Care

It is truly a challenge to bring a stranger into one's home and help the stranger to feel comfortable, relaxed, and motivated in order to create a positive and supportive environment for your child. Babies seem to do best with this kind of "one-to-one" relationship with a substitute caregiver. But when that arrangement is not feasible, there are many alternatives that have been tried and found to fit the needs of certain families. Following are some suggestions.

LIVE-IN "BARTER" ARRANGEMENTS

This is a combination of parental and substitute care. A single mother or father elects to live with another family that has a young child. The single parent receives living accommodations and meals in return for taking care of all children. In this way the single parent is able to act as primary caregiver for his or her own child, and at the same time supply continuity of care for the other child. Individual arrangements can vary; a small salary might be included, or the single parent may take on some part-time work at home.

COMMUNAL AND COOPERATIVE ARRANGEMENTS

Some families can form a communal or cooperative living arrangement in which two or three families occupy adjacent living quarters in a large house (or in neighboring homes or apartments) and care for one another's children. Providing they can be made to work without conflicts, these communal/cooperative arrangements can achieve the desired continuity despite the multiplicity of caregivers, since the children are cared for by persons with whom they have close daily contact. Parents who enter into this kind of arrangement (for the limited time we have discussed) will be mutually motivated to *make it work*.

FINANCIAL "POOLING" ARRANGEMENTS

By pooling their financial resources, two or three families can employ a full-time caregiver or caregivers. By careful selection they may be able to locate a nanny, or two nannies, or a nanny and an assistant, who will make the long-term commitment and provide the desired stability. This arrangement might seem at first to require substantial financial resources, but by sharing costs even families with modest incomes may be able to afford it, and even be able to pay an above average salary to a substitute.

GRANDPARENTS AND OTHER
MOTIVATED RELATIVES AND FRIENDS

Some grandparents may welcome the opportunity to help supervise the care of their infant and toddler grandchildren. Although there are often exceptions, many grandparents are strongly motivated to form and develop a close bond with their grandchildren. Factors such as health, lifestyles, motivation, and geography obviously play a part in whether or not grandparents are available for child care. But parents should consider using willing grandparents (or other relatives) as substitute caregivers on either a full-time or part-time basis. Some relatives seem instinctively to appreciate the need for continuity of care and may welcome the request. An added advantage is that grandparents may be a child-care resource that comes with little or no financial obligation. Even grandparents who do not have the desire, financial ability, or the good health to actually provide care can still be valuable by helping parents on occasion to observe and evaluate the care their grandchildren are receiving from paid caregivers.

Grandparents can be part-time, full-time, or supervising caregivers.

During my years as a psychotherapist I have been impressed by the love and devotion that grandparents have for their grandchildren. It is true that caring for these children demands time and vigilance. For the older person, this can be exhausting. But it is often so satisfying that grandparents willingly accept and sometimes even seek this task. The energy of grandparents can be conserved by using paid caregivers to work under their supervision. For the parent who must leave for work early in the morning, a paid caregiver could care for the children until grandma or grandpa arrives at 10:30 A.M. (or later).

In families where finances permit, the paid caregiver could remain the entire day, with the grandparent both supervising the caregiver and interacting with the grandchildren. There are several reasons why grandparents can be a most promising source of substitute care (either as "supervisors" of a substitute or as caregivers themselves). This applies not only to infants and toddlers but for older grandchildren as well:

- Each grandchild is a representation of their own immortality. They see and feel physical and psychological resemblances and connections. "Two-year-old Mary has her grandmother's smile!" Or, "Johnny has broad shoulders just like his football-playing uncle!" "Suzy is easygoing and reminds me of her grandpa."
- Grandparents can provide their grandchildren with the wisdom, time, and affection they might have been unable to show their own children due to the realistic pressures of daily living. With more leisure and insight, they can repair and augment the parenting role in a new way. Thus, the relationship between grandchild and grandparent becomes very special.
- It is also true that when grandparents retire from their work-a-day lives they have more time, and often more financial resources, to do such things as picking up an older grandchild at a nursery or elementary school, sharing the child's interests or hobbies, or taking part in other areas of the child's daily life. They can also provide a second home where the child feels safe, comfortable, and secure, and where the child can experience a new environment with different activities and equipment.

Parents may wish to consider the emotional impact on their child, as well as the practical aspects of providing substitute child care, as they contemplate the consequences of moving far away from involved grandparents. Grandparents should also stop and think before they move to a retirement community hundreds or thousands of miles away from grandchildren with whom they have established close bonds. Both generations can lose important relationships because of such a move! For when it comes to establishing a bond, a grandparent is no different than any other substitute caregiver. During the two or three years an infant and toddler receives care from grandparents, a close bond and attachment will usually form. If parents then move far from the grandparents, the child will usually feel a real loss. This may be true whether grandparents provided substitute care five days a week, two days, one day, or even if only on evenings or weekends. Whatever the depth of grandparent involvement, the severing of those ties may cause emotional distress to the child—just as might be expected from any other loss.

Americans today are a highly mobile people. Young parents frequently, almost routinely, move from one city to another as companies shift employees or parents change jobs. Grandparents and parents often relocate for a variety of reasons: better economic opportunities, better air, safer streets, more sunshine, better housing, a change of scenery, less cold weather, and so on. Retirement communities in places like Florida, North Carolina, Arizona, and California attract older citizens because of climate and recreational facilities. But young children and their interests are almost never considered when these moves are made. This is true not only for grandparents but also for other relatives—even close friends—who would ordinarily provide a valuable support system for young families. If mother and father live close enough to relatives and friends, the latter may be available for child care, or for help in finding substitutes. Parents who have moved to a distant city most likely have few friends, relatives, or other resources to call upon. Parents might want to think twice, therefore, before taking a job in a different community that will separate them from their family or other caring adults.

John and Sarah moved from their midwestern city to a new job for John in Los Angeles. Within a month after their arrival, their son Aaron was born. Sarah had no local relatives, and had not had time to develop any close friendships. Her mother did come to Los Angeles to help out but remained for only two weeks before she had to return to her commitments at home. Sarah was not only overwhelmed with her new responsibility as a mother; she also felt doubly stressed because of the absence of any support system of family and friends.

....

This lack of support system was further underscored when Sarah and John felt the need of additional income, which required Sarah to obtain outside employment. Had this occurred in her home city, her mother and other familiar persons would have been available to provide substitute care for Aaron. In addition, Sarah would have been able to share day care arrangements with her friends. All of this made the move to Los Angeles stressful particularly as she began to search for quality substitute care.

Sarah checked out several day-care facilities in her neighborhood that claimed to provide "quality" infant day care. She was appalled by what she saw—the large number of children involved and the much too large child-to-caregiver ratios. The facilities she looked at were, at best, custodial without any semblance of warm and responsive care.

Had Sarah and John delayed their move to Los Angeles until Aaron was age two, he would have had the opportunity to develop a secure emotional beginning. Sarah would have been far more able to handle the move and find suitable substitute care.

Of course this may mean that John would have had to forego an opportunity that was economically attractive. John might have seen it, at the time, as a decision that hampered his aspirations for early financial success and slowed his climb up the corporate ladder. But the trade-off for all three of them—Aaron, Sarah, and John—may have been well worth the price in years to come.

INCREASING THE PARENTAL ROLE AND REDUCING SUBSTITUTE CARE BY CUTTING JOB-RELATED TRAVEL TIME

Many parents today spend an inordinate amount of time commuting to and from work. In some sprawling cities, surrounded by equally sprawling residential suburbs, they spend two or more hours a day in cars, trains, or buses traveling to and from their jobs. Other parents, perhaps higher on the executive ladder, travel frequently to other cities for meetings or conventions that last for several days. All of this takes the parent away too much from the infant or toddler. Every hour that parents can be physically present with their infant or toddler is an hour that can help in the formation of a secure bond.

One possible way for parents to have extra time with their children is to try to reduce job travel time by working closer to home. If a job offer is so attractive that one is tempted to accept it despite having to put in many hours a week of travel time, there is another possible solution your child would appreciate: consider moving closer to your new job.

This may mean you will not enjoy the pleasures of a rural or suburban environment. But, the trade-off for your young child may be worth it. As we have discussed previously, your infant and toddler, at least in this critical period, needs his or her parents more than the child needs to experience an aesthetic environment with birds chirping and flowers blooming.

Furthermore, children benefit from parents who are not frazzled and exhausted by their commute. The fatigue created by an 80- or 90-minute drive on crowded streets or high-speed freeways can turn an otherwise loving and involved parent into an irritable and nonresponsive caregiver. Parents need to give such geographical considerations a second look.

"STANDARD" DAY CARE CENTER ARRANGEMENTS

In 1990 12 percent of the five million children under age three in substitute care were taken to day care or family care facilities.[5] These facilities vary greatly in both the quality of care and the amount of continuity provided. As pointed out in Chapter 4, we know from a recent University of California study that the turnover rate of caregivers in even the better day care centers exceeds 40 percent per year.[6] The "average" day care center probably has an even higher turnover rate. Nor is there any assurance that the same caregiver will care for the same child even on a daily or weekly basis. This severely impedes the attachment process. Even at the best day care centers an infant may be cared for by as many as six or more caregivers in one day!

As discussed in Chapter 4, the University of Colorado Public Report was highly critical of most center-based child care. This study further stated, "Despite the importance of good quality child care, only one in seven centers provided a level of child care quality that promotes healthy development and learning."[7]

> *A recent study found that only 14% of childcare centers provide acceptable care.*

Parents should be aware, too, that children in day-care centers face several other problems that may not at first be apparent. For example, there is a greatly increased risk of illness since a child is exposed to so many other children, as well as numerous caregivers.

Another concern with day care is the large number of children involved. This makes supervision and individual attention more difficult to provide than within a home setting. Infants and toddlers may experience increased stress and abuse from other children.

On the positive side, at better day care centers—particularly those that are university-based or industry-based—supervision and training is usually of better quality.

It is important that parents appreciate the fact that the quality of child care is primarily related to staff-to-child ratios, staff education, and administrators' experience. The education of staff should include specialized courses in early childhood, education and in developmental psychology. Higher wages for staff help should be paid to insure less rapid turnover, as well as attracting better qualified personnel. Moreover, such facilities are usually licensed, assuring parents of at least minimum standards of care and training of personnel. This is not necessarily true for the many unlicensed child care facilities. Parents may wish to think carefully before placing very young children in such facilities, which may not achieve even minimal standards.

Having said all this, and realizing how hard it is to find quality care, it is possible to find centers that will provide what the child needs if day care must be used. Remember, however, that the search must be made for one of the 14 percent of centers that do provide developmentally appropriate care, since there is convincing evidence that most do not.[8]

This 14 percent of "developmentally appropriate" care provided by some centers was calculated using a well-known rating scale. To be included in this appropriate range, centers had to score "5" or more, which the rating defined as "good," with the following criteria:

- Health and safety needs are fully met;
- staff are caring and supportive of children;
- children are learning in many ways through interesting, fun activities.

A score of "7," which equals an excellent rating, adds that:

- Children are encouraged to become independent;
- the teacher plans for individual learning needs; and
- adults have close personal relationships with each child.

Sadly, 86 percent of the 401 centers studied failed to meet these standards.[9]

The researchers also expressed grave concern over their findings that the quality in rooms caring for infants and toddlers was substantially lower than rooms caring for older children. Only 8 percent met the high quality level. Ninety-two percent received a rating of poor to mediocre. Of this number, 40 percent had poor quality (a rating below three). For infant/toddlers, such a score (below 3) indicates that the health and welfare of these very young and vulnerable children are at a substantial risk during the long hours they spend in the centers. These poor quality infant/toddler rooms are typified by a lack of basic sanitary conditions for diapering and feeding. There is a lack of warm, supportive relationships with caring adults—children

92% of all infant and toddler facilities fail to meet minimum standards.

are rarely held, cuddled or talked to. There is little or no use of toys and other materials that encourage physical, social and emotional growth.[10] Therefore, parents should carefully investigate and observe child-care centers before enrolling their children, particularly if some of the other arrangements discussed in this chapter do not seem feasible.

Unfortunately, when visiting a day-care center, it is easier to observe the physical plant, the equipment, and the caregiver-to-child ratio than it is to learn about the subjective quality of the caregiving. It is hard to observe what goes on during feeding, diapering, or the time that an infant is put to sleep. This is especially true if the parent is walked through with the director or other personnel. Often, the parent is anxious that his or her child be accepted and feels reluctant to ask the hard questions or demand an extended observation time. Centers with good reputations or that are connected to universities often have long waiting lists and admission may be difficult. Perhaps these considerations explain why the University of Colorado study previously mentioned concluded that parents, in evaluating child-care centers, "dramatically over-estimated the quality of care their children were receiving."[11] Parents want to "feel good" about the facility to whom they entrust their child. They do not want to have disturbing doubts.

In view of these considerations, it is definitely desirable that the parent considering any day-care center (or any other facility) ask permission to quietly sit "out of the way" and simply watch what goes on, as suggested by Dr. Benjamin Spock.[12] One need not be an expert to determine if the care is kind, thoughtful, and nurturing (or otherwise). If permissible, such observation should be conducted over at least one hour if not more. Very little information can be obtained in five or ten minutes.

"FAMILY CARE" ARRANGEMENTS

In 1990 11.2 percent of the five million children under age three in substitute care were enrolled in a "family care" facility.[13] Typically, this is a private home, often unlicensed, where four or five children are cared for by one or two persons, whose qualifications may be difficult to evaluate. It is extremely hard to predict the quality and continuity of care at such facilities. Unfortunately, when they are licensed, on-site observation of these facilities occurs very infrequently—once every three years or less—as in California, Connecticut, Iowa, New York, Pennsylvania, and Texas.[14] The training and supervision of the child-care personnel is often poor. Once again, parents should investigate such facilities carefully. I have observed enormous differences in the physical environment, play equipment, and in staff training at such family care centers. A final note: infants and toddlers in both day-care facilities and in family care arrangements are subjected to the additional daily disruption of leaving their familiar home environment—often from early in the morning until five or six in the evening (or later).

Criteria for Selection of Day Care and Family Care

It is just as imperative to investigate day-care and family care facilities as it is to investigate an individual nanny. One would assume that the personnel involved in the administration and direction of day-care centers, particularly the better university-based centers, would make a careful investigation of day-care personnel before they are employed. Indeed, research indicates that some investigation is almost always done to screen out those who are patently unqualified. But the investigative process and the judgment as to who is and is not employed is so subjective that it is advisable for parents to do some checking on their own.

Here are some questions you may wish to ask before placing your child in a facility away from your own home.

1. *What Is the Infant-to-Caregiver Ratio?* Be specific in asking. For example, "At 10:00 A.M." (or at other specific times) "how many infants are cared for by each caregiver?" The recommended maximum ratio, according to Dr. Benjamin Spock, is no more than three infants under

one year of age per caregiver.[15] The reason is that with infants, unlike older children, needs should be promptly addressed. Their capacity to wait for satisfaction is greatly reduced. Delay in meeting their needs creates anxiety and interferes with the development of the bond between child and adult. Remember that the longer and louder a child must cry when distressed, the harder it is for the infant to create a positive feeling that the world is a satisfying place and that he or she is valued and loved.

2. *What Is the Rate of Turnover of Caregivers?* Many children spend 8 to 12 hours per day at day-care facilities. During this period, how many different people will interact with your child? The more persons to whom your child must relate to, the more difficult it will be for him or her to establish the necessary secure attachment, and to be able to develop a trusting relationship. This is especially true for infants and toddlers who thrive on predictability.

It is therefore important to question how many caregivers have arrived and departed during the past two years. Some caregivers are students who leave after a semester, having fulfilled some academic or work requirement. Others use the experience to further their career into better paying jobs. As mentioned, the annual turnover rate at university-based centers is over 40 percent, but this statistic does not include the caregiver changes that occur in the average care center's day.[16] For example, during a typical day workers' hours are staggered; there are coffee breaks, lunch breaks, and shift changes. As a result, an infant can be cared for by as many as six or more different people during the child's 8- to 10-hour stay at the center. It is difficult to develop a secure attachment when so relatively little time is spent with any one person. Contrast this with the one-to-one relationship between a parent and his or her infant when mother or father have most of the week to interact.

One diplomatic method of inquiry is to ask "How many persons will actually care for my child? Will one person be assigned to my child and remain with him or her during the entire day?"

Further disruption often occurs in the child's attachment to caregivers when the child becomes too old for the infant group and moves on to the toddler group. Here, again, new personnel are introduced to the child as he or she begins to walk and become more exploratory.

Ironically, even in the best day-care centers, it is very difficult for the infant or toddler to develop a secure attachment to any *one* caregiver. This may be true regardless of a very favorable staff-to-child ratio at such centers. As has been stated earlier in the book, it takes time and the predictability of hundreds of interactions before a secure attachment is achieved with any one person. It is also ironic, and underappreciated, that the same day-care center, with well-trained personnel, age-appropriate play equipment, and a small teacher-to-child ratio, is an excellent environment for the two- to four-year-old child and provides a rich, social, and educational experience. However, the opposite may be

An optimum environment for a 3-year-old may be damaging for an infant or toddler.

true for the preverbal infant and toddler, whose most important developmental task is the formation of a predictable and trusting relationship. This is very difficult to achieve with multiple changing caregivers; even with those caregivers who have excellent training and supervision. Of course, training and supervision are important to insure optimum care of physical needs and prevent many health problems from developing. It is also true that a well-supervised center will encourage more immediate interaction with your infant or toddler.

3. *What are the hiring procedures for day-care personnel?*
When a child-care center employs personnel to care for its charges, most of the same considerations should

apply that were discussed previously for the selection of a "nanny." However, one obvious additional factor is that the center (as well as the parent) must consider the educational background, degrees (if any), and general qualifications of the center employees who engage in this important work. A parent will usually find that more highly qualified, trained, and educated personnel are found at child-care centers operated by major universities or large corporations as compared with commercial or private care centers. Also, university care centers will usually be more sophisticated and selective in their hiring techniques as well as in supervision of its employees once hiring has occurred.

Of course, when evaluating a care center it would be impractical to go through the detailed inquiry that was suggested earlier in this chapter for hiring nannies because the questions raised there would undoubtedly be irritating (to say the least) to persons in charge of a university care center.

4. *What screening is carried out to make decisions on the admission of children?* Parents may wish to know whether or not the care center under consideration admits autistic, retarded, emotionally disturbed, or otherwise handicapped children. If admitted, are there specialized personnel available to deal with the special needs of these children? Extremely aggressive children can terrify a toddler who is separated from his or her parents and who feels little protection from care givers. A toddler may be overwhelmed by the intensity of the rage expressed by an angry child. Even if the anger or aggression is not directed at the child itself, the witnessing of disturbed behavior in another child can be extremely upsetting.

Therefore, it is of interest to find out how much information parents are asked to provide about the child's history and family background before the child is accepted by the center. Parents should note what forms are used and what interviews or observations of the child take place before admission. This will help the parents to determine if the center will be in a position to evaluate and meet the specialized needs of each child admitted.

David and Susan enrolled their 15-month-old John at a day-care center on a Saturday. They met the director and one teacher. They did not observe the other children in John's group, who ranged in age from one to two and a half years. The facilities looked clean, cheerful, and had age-appropriate toys and equipment. Unfortunately, two of the six children there were extremely aggressive. One was a "biter"; when he wanted a toy, he would bite another child in order to obtain it. Even though John himself was not attacked, the wails and screams of the two year old who was bitten frightened him and made the transition to the center extremely difficult.

Clearly, it would have been helpful, before John was enrolled, to have observed the behavior of the other children with whom John would be grouped.

5. *What are the health provisions of the center?* If an infant brought in by another parent is coughing, or develops a fever during the day, what provision if any is made to isolate the sick child to prevent spread of the illness to other children? Is there an isolation room or sick corner provided? When diapers are changed, what hygienic procedures are followed? What means are taken to prevent the "sharing" of bottles, pacifiers, and infant toys to prevent the spread of infection among the young children at the center? What is the procedure if an emergency develops? If the child falls or is injured or

becomes ill, is a doctor or emergency hospital nearby? Will a parent be called? It is advisable to find out if the facility does have a protocol of some type (written or oral) that addresses these concerns and if it sounds reasonable and logical.

MEDICAL RISKS OF DAY CARE

There is much research on this subject. "There is a large and growing body of evidence that day care is a breeding ground for *infectious diseases*. The mere act of separating an infant from his mother may suppress the immune system and make the child more vulnerable to disease."[17] (emphasis added)

A 1989 study compared the infection rate, need for medical care, and medical costs of children at home to children in day care. The study found that children in day care, whether family care or at centers were at much greater risk to contract infections.

> *Parents are seldom aware of increased risks of illness and accidents in daycare.*

Day-care centers were clearly the most dangerous; children in these facilities were "nearly three times as likely to need hospitalization." Furthermore, the cost of medical care for children in day care was two to three times the cost compared to children cared for at home.[18]

Children cared for at day-care centers are also at greater risk to develop bronchitis and pneumonia as well as gastrointestinal infections.[19] Even more unfortunate is the "snowballing effect" that occurs when such children fall ill. Their illness then spreads not only to those who work at the centers, but also to the homes of such workers and the homes of the children who became ill. Such outbreaks are not isolated; they recur regularly.[20]

In addition to the diseases mentioned, children in day care are also more likely to contract skin infections and other invasive bacterial diseases such as meningitis. This disease may either kill or cause permanent damage to children.[21] Another disturbing study indicated that "Children in daycare are at a 50% to 100% increased risk for contracting [certain] fatal and maiming diseases for each year in daycare."[22]

Not only does a sick infant cause stress and worry for concerned parents, such illness usually has additional cost: one parent usually stays home and loses wages in order to care for the baby or toddler when ill. Frequently, the mom or dad or other sibling will catch the cold of the coughing or sneezing child. This may well increase the time loss from work as well as cause added medical, hospital, and prescription costs for the entire family.

Parents might wish to consider these hidden risks when enrolling their infant in a group facility.

....

6. *Do parents have the right to "drop in" unannounced?* This would afford you the opportunity to obtain information that can help you to verify, to a significant degree, what goes on at the facility. For example, in some day-care centers a visitor can see how many persons care for each child, and what the children are doing. Other facilities—perhaps with a more elaborate layout—make it impossible to observe unless one is ushered past the entrance into a working area. No valid observation can be made unless the parent is able to see specifically what goes on as the children are handled by and interact with the caregivers.

Assuming that the parent is allowed to "drop in" and observe, he or she should take note of how much crying is going on, what the noise level is, and assess the general atmosphere in the environment. The parent can tell whether all appears to be quiet and tranquil, and whether the infants are played with, fed, and otherwise cared for well. Parents may feel reassured if they observe such an atmosphere. However, if the parent sees that several babies are left to cry unattended during the five or ten minutes of the visit, this should be a matter of serious concern regardless of what "explanations" are given.

It is advisable to make this kind of investigation *before* deciding to enroll your infant. Formal licensing requirements demand very little: government inspection is minimal and in some areas almost nonexistent. Prior to actual enrollment, therefore, it is suggested that parents spend at least a full morning or afternoon quietly and unobtrusively watching how staff care for the children. Dr. Benjamin Spock suggests that parents should visit a prospective day-care facility "several times" for "several hours" so that they are able "to see the quality of care."[23]

If the facility refuses to let the parent make an unannounced on-site visitation once the child is enrolled, or refuses to let the parent spend a morning or an afternoon observing before enrollment, other facilities should be considered.

7. *What play facilities and equipment are available?* Toys, books, paint, clay, sand, water equipment, blocks, and other developmentally important equipment should be available, especially for toddlers. Some facilities may avoid the use of certain of these items—usually paint or clay—because they create a mess. The use of these items requires more intense supervision and cleanup work. But experience in a variety of these materials is so essential for young children that parents may

wish to select a facility that does provide for their use, and rule out one that places neatness and orderliness above the need for the creative experiences all children require.

For the toddler and preschool child, blocks, puzzles, musical instruments, and dress-up and housekeeping equipment should be readily available to stimulate and enrich the hours away from home. It is important to question the extent to which television and videos are used during the week. Time spent sitting and watching television is now actively scheduled in many centers instead of the more preferable supervised play. Parents often are not informed as to the programs shown.

Regarding playground equipment, parents should observe and determine if the swings are safe. For example, bucket swings which supply front and rear protection for both infants and toddlers should be available. The parents should further determine if there is sufficient room for the swings, themselves, so that children do not accidentally walk into them. What protective surfaces are provided under climbing and other equipment? Such protective surfaces might include mats, grass, dirt, and so on.

8. *Will parents be allowed to participate in the transition period.* No matter who the substitute caregivers may be—nanny, baby-sitter, day-care or family care workers—parents should make every effort not only to observe the child in the caregiving environment but also to take the time to be physically present during the "transition" period, which we can arbitrarily fix at any time from a few days to a week or perhaps even a few weeks.

During this time the parent, along with the substitute, will interact with the infant or toddler. This will facilitate development of a positive relationship between the child and the substitute because of the added feeling of security the parental presence provides.

Separation from the familiar caregiver and adjusting to new personnel and environment varies with each child. Many children make the transition more smoothly if they are encouraged to bring bottles, pacifiers, stuffed animals, or a favorite blanket to the center to serve as a transitional object at nap time, or when the child is upset. If center personnel do not themselves suggest this, the parent can do so.

If the parent is not allowed to participate in a transitional period this way but is required to drop off the child "cold turkey," the facility should be avoided. As we saw when our young friend Timmy was dropped off at a family day-care center without explanation or preparation, it was most upsetting and traumatic for him. At all ages, separations can be difficult; but they are especially hard for the preverbal child who cannot be prepared for change.

Parents may be reluctant to ask some of the questions suggested above. They may worry that their inquiries will be interpreted as an implicit criticism of the facility. And no doubt that some of the child-care and family care personnel may be annoyed, or even reluctant, to answer these concerns. But the best interests of your child mandate inquiry into these various areas. A well-run child-care facility will ordinarily be willing to see to it that the questions are answered fully. If the facility is unwilling to supply the information, a warning flag should go up!

Will One of the Alternative Arrangements Be Practical for You?

Some of these alternative arrangements may seem feasible to you. Others may seem futile or impractical. However, each of them has been used successfully by parents. For example, if parents need only four hours a day of substitute care, five days a week, the need for continuity of care is less critical since the child is physically in the parent's care most of his or her waking hours. So even if there are frequent changes of substitute caregivers during these 20 hours per week, the emotional impact of such changes is far less than the impact on a child in day care for 40 or more hours per week. In considering the alternatives, parents need to keep in mind the "mix" of parental and substitute care best suited to each family's different needs.

Final Thoughts on "Being There"

The young mother lies exhausted but exhilarated, on the delivery table. Her new infant—her first child—lies quietly content, cradled against her body. The doctor busies himself cutting the umbilical cord. The masked and gowned father stares in wondrous relief, the magic words still ringing in his ears "You have a healthy baby girl."

Later, both mother and father confess to having had similar thoughts at that moment: what can I do in the months and years ahead to be the best possible parent to this tiny, miraculous child? And, at that moment, both parents resolve to do whatever is necessary to protect, nurture, and guide their daughter.

This young couple will soon find that having a baby is at once the greatest joy, the biggest intrusion, and the source of the most dramatic change in their life. Unfortunately, most of us are unprepared for this new role. Few of us have had the experience of growing up in a large family where we could learn about child-care responsibilities. And there is so little time to practice the skills and arts of being the kind of parent we all want to be. The nearly universal reaction reported by new mothers and fathers is astonishment at how much work is involved in infant care and how one's life is so completely changed by the new arrival. Yet the baby cannot be sent back. We cannot trade our child for a "new model" or, as with a job, change it when it proves too stressful. In essence, we cannot divorce a child!

The baby comes with enormous needs. The newborn is an individual who cannot understand the outside world, whose communications are nonverbal and primitive, and who is totally dependent. In turn, babies are greeted by parents who themselves are virtually unprepared for this new role. The parents may also be concerned about avoiding making with their child the mistakes their parents made while caring for them.

In past decades, most formal preparation for parenting came from childbirthing classes where the focus was on the mother: on her delivery and on helping her to breast-feed. Little time was devoted to the infant and his or her needs, or to expected developmental changes, or to the importance of the attachment process. Yet, preparing in these ways for the coming of the baby would certainly make all of us better able to cope with the newness of the parenting experience. Any kind of support group for new parents would indeed help. Surely it behooves society to take a hand in this preparation. Mandated classes in high school and college on infant and child care and development (for both males and females) may be a first step in respecting and focusing on the needs of the new baby. These classes may be just as important as algebra, American literature, physical education, or history in preparing a young person to cope with adult life.

It is also true that the reason the parenting process is so difficult is because one must be responsive not only to each child as an individual, but also to the constant shifts and changes in the child's development and behavior. Parents need to appreciate their child's growth, acknowledging that each stage and each developmental task has value. Thus the exploratory needs of toddlers may be just as important and require just as much attention as the later academic struggles and pressures of the school-age child. Parents must learn the value of close physical contact with their newborn—just as they must learn to step back, in later years, to allow the teenager his or her privacy.

Not only are there inadequate supports and programs to help make parents ready for their new roles as mom and dad, there are virtually *no advocates* for infants and toddlers themselves. Every other segment of society has its own interest group. Every trade and industrial union has lobbyists or political action committees to zealously protect its interests. The feminist movement has its highly articulate advocates. Consumer groups, artists, professional organizations—all have effective spokespersons. There are five times the number of animal rights groups as there are groups that focus even tangentially on infants and toddlers. Our leaders of tomorrow—the infants and toddlers of today—have little in the way of support groups to speak for and protect *their* interests. Some child psychologists feel that child impact statements should be required with planning or licensing applications or in connection with new regulations or laws. Of course, the requirement of a child impact statement may seem unimportant in comparison with other contemporary problems. But isn't the welfare of children as valuable as the height of buildings, population density, and the preservation of wildlife?

Because preverbal children have no voice, we must awaken our leadership, as well as parents, to recognize and deal with the issues that concern the unique needs of infants and toddlers. Who will cry out and express the pain, hunger, and fear of these children who have no language, who are helpless and powerless? Who will respond to their cries when they are victims of caregiver roulette and cannot learn to feel safe and secure?

When Bowlby was asked, "What do children need to grow up to feel happy and secure?" he answered, "They need a mother figure who will care for them. She doesn't have to be on duty day in, day out. If she can get some assistance from her own mother, her husband, or one of her own sisters, the more help she gets, the better. But they should be responsible for their own children. They should be the principal caregiver. And if they are not the principal caregiver, then they must try and find someone else who will be. Someone who plays that major role through the child's childhood."[1]

It is not my intent to condemn all substitute care (day care, family care, or nanny care). But significant amounts of money and effort need to be spent to upgrade day care centers, and to raise all child-care standards. Training and on-site supervision *are* vital to safeguard our children. We need to support more industries in their efforts to provide day care for their workers' children and to pay more than the minimum wage for caregivers. These caregivers also need to stay with each child through infancy and the toddler years to provide the much-needed continuity.

But we should always keep in mind the real differences between young children (infants and toddlers) and their older counterparts. For the older child, the institutions mentioned—family care and day care—at industry, private, and university facilities can provide important social and play experiences that are enriching, stimulating, and necessary for healthy development. But my concern is that these institutional experiences, while appropriate for children two and a half years and older, are not the best places for infants and toddlers. Even for three and four year olds, the 50-plus hours per week spent away from (working) parents create their own stress. However, older children, with language ability, can be heard and comforted; their problems can be discussed and their positions supported.

Another example where developmental differences must be respected is in toilet training. Most children usually learn to use the potty or toilet by the end of the second year, or certainly during the third year. But expecting a child to master toilet training in the first six months of life is difficult and contraindicated. We also know that the two year old can be weaned from breast or bottle, but at two or three months of age a baby still needs the sucking that is provided by nursing.

It is also common knowledge that puppies and kittens should be kept with their mothers until they reach a critical point in their development when they can survive independently. We would not consider taking a puppy, calf, or foal from its mother and giving it to another animal to suckle.

Puppies and kittens are kept with their mothers; why not infants?

Yet many educated and sophisticated parents fail to appreciate removing an infant from its mother, and placing it in an institutional setting, is not only inappropriate but may be detrimental to infant development.

Substitute care in the form of nannies, housekeepers, day and family care personnel, and others *can* provide appropriate nurturing. But we know that today, the reality is that most caregivers change so often that this kind of care can be wildly inconsistent. In fact, caregiver roulette undermines the emotional health of the children involved, since the lack of continuity prevents the development of trust and formation of the essential secure attachment. All child-care experts emphasize the importance of quality care either at day-care facilities, in family care or with in-house nannies. Quality care should mean consistency, stability, continuity, and individualized attention as well as warm and responsive interactions between child and caregiver.

It would be far different if society could rely upon a stable family unit to give our children, both young and old, the strong emotional base we all need. Mothers need either a father's help, or someone to nurture them as well. But we do not have a stable society with extended families and neighbors who, as in the past, can help young families to provide such an emotional base.

One of my motivations for writing this book is my increasing concern that economic and social forces are simply overwhelming young parents, and causing their children to end up as the real victims.

In this book I am trying to raise a voice that will encourage parents to appreciate the value of making an investment of their time and presence in the early years of their child's life. My intent is to raise the consciousness of new parents at a time when society seems to neglect the needs of the very young. The following example illustrates how a young mother recently resolved her caregiving dilemma by making such an investment in her young child:

Bonny, a new mother, was confronted with a dilemma that so many parents face today. She had been offered a teaching assignment to begin when her baby was five months old. At the same time she was encouraged by family and friends to find good substitute care for her baby Laura and to take advantage of both the money and career experience offered by the teaching position. However, after several discussions she became aware of the impact on her baby if she returned to work. She also recognized the importance of the bonding experience, and the irreversible effects of multiple caregivers early in the child's life. In spite of pressure from friends, she decided to follow her own instinctual feelings about caring for her infant. These feelings were strong enough to motivate her to forego, temporarily, her teaching opportunity in favor of being a full-time committed parent.

It was both her maternal feelings coupled with some rational and intellectual insight that she gained from discussions dealing with her problem that helped her to arrive at this difficult decision and to temporarily resolve her dilemma until her child was older.

It is because children are—or can be—a source of enormous pleasure, wonder, laughter, awe, and love that I wish to encourage mothers and fathers to participate fully in the parenting process. I also want to emphasize that these commitments to one's developing child are *as important as any career* for the limited time we are privileged to be parents.

There is no doubt that parental stimulation, supervision, and concern can add to the growing experience of the child at any age. But most important is the fact of *being there*. Simple parental presence at all ages can provide a secure base that frees the child to explore, to learn, to relate to others, and to master his or her world—first as a child and later as an adult. The positive effects of a parent being there continue throughout life.

Being there, however, does not mean always acting as the *ideal* parent. Every mother is at times preoccupied, at times irritable, at times sad, at times silly, at times angry and explosive, and at other times nonresponsive. But being there allows the child to learn what a parent is like without the child having an underlying concern of abandonment. Being there, providing continuity and responsive care in the early years has lifelong benefits, not only to the individual child but as a way to help alleviate many of our society's ills.

In talking with older men and women in the past, I have found their reminiscences are amazingly similar: many regret the fact that they spent so little time with their children, compared with time they spent on their business or professional careers. Others rejoice in fond memories of their family life, and are grateful for those relationships and attachments in which they did invest time and effort.

In the end, it was the experiences of being there that really mattered.

A MOTHER REMEMBERS

A mother might reflect and remember:
I was there to feel the excitement of birth: the strange lights, the exploring hands, the waves of pain, the embarrassment of body fluids; I was the center of a solar system; the severing of our biological connector, images of a gray slippery entity, a sudden cry, a pink fist, open eyes, damp hair, and the weight of a baby laid on my heart.

I was there to soothe her to sleep, to nurse with pins and needles in my breast, to bask in her contentment, to worry with her distress, to melt with her smiles, and babble with her coos.

I was there to feel the panic of his first rash, a watery stool, a sudden fever, a poor weight gain, and then to feel calmed by the experienced and the wise.

I was there to feel the warmth of a snuggle, the torment of exhaustion, the disruption of household order, and the worry that there was no light at the end of the tunnel.

I was there to wipe, diaper, oil, powder and bathe; to pace, jostle, stroke, and pat; to croon, moan, and cry.

I was there to push her swing in the air, to watch her pour sand from her bucket, to pick up the dumped crayons, and to say "no" to a dangerous climb.

I was there to empty his potty, to help him hold on to his teddy, to comfort his night terror, and to giggle with his nonsense.

I was there for the first day of school, to feel the clutching, the panic, her bravery and concern, to feel the slow transfer of trust as her world grew.

I was there to sympathize with a disappointment, a rejection, a loss, and a hurt; to read, to sing, to laugh, to teach and explain.

I was there to scold, yell, be irritable; to feel guilty and to apologize.

I was there to feel her new power; her wider world of ideas, skills, and mastery.

I was there to meet his new friends and allies, to acknowledge his growing need for independence and privacy, to feel his anger and his rage.

I was there to celebrate; to congratulate, to drive, and to cook; sharing holidays, birthdays, and moments of joy.

I was there . . .

Notes

CHAPTER 1: WHO CARES FOR OUR CHILDREN: A PARENT'S DILEMMA

1. Carnegie Corporation of New York, *Starting Points—Meeting the Needs of Our Youngest Children* (New York: Carnegie Corp., 1994).
2. *Ibid*. p. vii.
3. *Ibid*. p. 106.
4. Daniel Stern, *Diary of a Baby*, (New York: Basic Books, 1990), pp. 92–93.
5. Penelope Leach, *Children First: What Our Society Must Do And Is Not Doing For Our Children* (New York: Alfred Knopf, 1994) p. 88.
6. *Ibid*. p. 206.
7. L. Alan Sroufe, et al., *Child Development: Its Nature and Course*, 2nd ed (New York: McGraw Hill, 1992) p. 217.
8. John Bowlby, "Forty-Four Juvenile Thieves: Their Characters and Home Life"; *Inter. J. of Psychoanalysis* 25: pp. 19–52, 107–127 (Reprint, (Monograph) Gordon Bailiere, Tindall & Cox, 1946).
9. Carnegie, *Starting Points*, p. 76.
10. John Bowlby, A Secure Base (New York: Basic Books, 1988), p. 46.
11. R. A. Spitz, "Hospitalism: An Inquiry into the Genesis of Psychiatric Conditions in Early Childhood," *Psychoanalytic Study of the Child*, (1945): pp. 53–74.
12. S. J. Suomi and H. F. Harlow, "Abnormal Social Behavior in Young Monkeys," in *Exceptional Infant*, Vol. 2, ed. J. Helmuth (New York: Bruner/Mazel, 1971).
13. Carnegie, *Starting Points*, p. x.
14. *Ibid*. p. xiii.
15. *Ibid*. p. 43.

16. Jay Belsky, "Infant Day Care: A Cause for Concern?" *Zero to Three* (Special Reprint of Article, September 1986), p. 6.

CHAPTER 2: GIVING THE GIFT OF LOVE: PARENTHOOD AS A TEMPORARY CAREER

1. Dr. Benjamin Spock, *A Better World for Our Children* (Bethesda: National Press Books, 1994) p. 142.
2. Leach, *Children First*, p. xv.
3. Margaret Thatcher, interview by Larry King, *The Larry King Show*, Cable News Network, June 26, 1995.
4. Harriet Heath, "A Good Reference for Parents," *Zero to Three* (Special Reprint, Feb. 1987 article): p. 25.
5. Jay Belsky, "Risks Remain," *Zero to Three* (Special Reprint including "Infant Day Care" Articles through June, 1987): p. 22.
6. Leach, *Children First*, p. 78.
7. *Ibid.* p. 78.
8. Carnegie, *Starting Points*, p. 95.
9. *Ibid.* p. 6.

CHAPTER 3: BONDING AND ATTACHMENT: THE KEY TO UNDERSTANDING PARENT-INFANT BEHAVIOR

1. Carnegie, *Starting Points*, p. 45.
2. Bowlby, *Attachment and Loss*, vol. 1, *Attachment* (New York: Basic Books, 1969), pp. 240–241.
3. Magid and McKelvey, *High Risk: Children Without a Conscience*, (New York: Bantam Books, 1988), pp. 67–68.
4. Leach, *Children First*, p. 55.
5. M. Konner, "The Enigmatic Smile," *Psychology Today* (March 1987): pp. 42–44, quoted in Magid and McKelvey, *High Risk: Children Without a Conscience*, p. 247.
6. Bowlby, *A Secure Base*, Bowlby, *Attachment and Loss*, vol. 1, *Attachment* pp. 80–82; Bowlby, *Attachment and Loss*, vol. 2, *Separation*, p. 203.

7. Bowlby, *Attachment and Loss*, vol. 2, *Separation*, p. 208.
8. Selma Fraiberg, Lecture at Univ. of Calif., San Francisco, 1981.
9. Mary Ainsworth, *Infancy in Uganda: Infant Care and the Growth of Love*, (Maryland: Johns Hopkins University Press, 1967), p. 345.
10. Daniel Stern, *Diary of a Baby*, (New York: Basic Books, 1990), pp. 92–93.
11. Bowlby, *A Secure Base*, p. 11.
12. *Ibid.* p. 12.
13. Carnegie, *Starting Points*, p. vii.
14. Ainsworth, et al., *Patterns of Attachment: A Psychological Study of the Strange Situation* (Hillsdale, N.J.: Erlbaum, 1978).
15. L. Alan Sroufe and E. Waters, "Heart Rate as a Convergent Measure in Clinical and Developmental Research, *Merrill-Palmer Quarterly* 23 (1977): pp. 3–27.
16. Bowlby, *A Secure Base*, (1988) pp. 126–128.
17. J. Robertson, *A Two Year Old Goes to the Hospital*. (University Park, Pennsylvania: Pennsylvania State Audio Visual Services, 1953) films.
18. J. Robertson, *Guide to Film—A Two Year Old Goes to the Hospital*, 3d ed. (Tavistock Child Development Research, 1965) cited in John Bowlby, *Attachment and Loss*, vol. 3, Loss, Sadness and Depression (New York: Basic Books, 1980), p. 10.
19. Bowlby, *A Secure Base*, p. 62.

CHAPTER 4: WHAT HAPPENS WHEN CAREGIVERS CHANGE: THE DANGERS OF "CAREGIVER ROULETTE"

1. Dr. T. Berry Brazelton on ABC's "Oprah Winfrey Show" on May 16, 1995.
2. Children's Defense Fund, *The State of America's Children Yearbook*, (Washington, D.C.: Children's Defense Fund, 1995).
3. *Ibid.* p. 72.
4. Carnegie, *Starting Points,* p. 88.

5. Marcy Whitebook, Carollee Howes, and Deborah Phillips, *Who Cares? Child Care Teachers and the Quality of Care in America*, Child Care Employee Project of the National Child Care Staffing Study (Washington, D.C.: Child Care Employee Project, 1989): p. 12.

6. Statement by Marcy Whitebook, Director of the National Child Care Staffing Study, Pat Wingert and Barbara Kantrowitz, "The Day Care Generation," *Newsweek Special Issue*, (Winter/Spring 1990): p. 92.

7. Carnegie, *Starting Points*, p. 55.

8. *Ibid.* p. 55.

9. Leach, *Children First*, p. 80.

10. Edward Zigler, Yale Bush Center, telephone conversation with author on July 18, 1995.

11. Univ. of Colorado, Denver, *Cost, Quality and Child Outcomes in Child Care Centers*, 2d ed. (Denver: Univ. of Colorado, Denver, Economics Department, 1995): p. 26.

12. *Ibid.* p. 73.

13. *Ibid.* p. 28.

14. White, "Should You Stay Home With Your Baby?" *American Baby* (1985): pp. 27–28, 30, quoted in Magid and McKelvey, *High Risk*, p. 134.

15. Jay Belsky, "Infant Daycare and Socioeconomic Development," *The United States Journal of Psychology and Psychiatry* 29, no. 4 (1988): pp. 379–406; Jay Belsky, "Effects of Infant Day Care Reconsidered," *Early Childhood Research Quarterly* (1988) pp. 235, 265, 266.

16. Carollee Howes, and P. Stewart, (1986). *Child's Play with Adults, Peers and Toys*. Unpublished manuscript, University of California at Los Angeles. Summarized and discussed in *Zero to Three*—Special Reprint of Feb., 1987 article: Selective Review of Infant Day Care Research: A Cause for Concern by Deborah Phillips, Kathleen McCartney, Sandra Scarr and Carollee Howes. Publisher: National Center for Clinical Infant Program, Arlington, Va.

17. L. Alan Sroufe, et al., *Child Development: Its Nature and Course*, p. 221.

18. Carnegie, *Starting Points*, p. 5.
19. Jay Belsky, "Infant Day Care: A Cause for Concern," *Zero to Three*, (Special Reprint of Article, September 1986), p. 7.
20. M. Erickson, L. A. Sroufe, and B. Egeland, *The Relationship Between Quality of Attachment and Behavior Problems In Preschool In a High Risk Sample*, (Monographs for the Society for Research in Child Development, 1985), p. 162.
21. *Ibid.* p. 149.
22. John Bowlby, *The Making and Breaking of Affectional Bonds*, (London: Tavistock Publications, 1979). pp. 127–160.
23. John L. Weil, *Early Deprivation of Empathic Care*, (Madison, Conn.: International Universities Press, 1992), p. 113.
24. Carollee Howes, University of California Study, reported in Pat Wingert and Barbara Kantrowitz, "The Day Care Generation," *Newsweek Special Issue*, Winter/Spring 1990 p. 92.
25. University of North Carolina—(Frances Parker Study) reported by Haskins, R.: *Public School Aggression Amongst Children With Varying Day-care Experience*— Child Development 56—pp. 689–703; also reported in *Zero to Three* Special Reprint—(p. 6) Sept. 1986 Article by Belsky, J. and in the *Zero to Three* Child Care Anthology (1984–1992) by the National Center for Clinical Infant Programs, Arlington, Va (1992), p. 113.
26. Jay Belsky, "Infant Day Care: A Cause for Concern" *Zero to Three*, (Special Reprint of Article, September 1986), p. 6.
27. *Ibid*.
28. Magid and McKelvey, *High Risk*, p. 4.
29. *Ibid*.
30. Emmy Werner, "High Risk Children In Young Adulthood," *American Journal of Orthopsychiatry* 59-1 (January 1989): pp. 75 and 76.

31. Magid and McKelvey, *High Risk*, p. 246.
32. *Ibid.* p. 189.
33. *Ibid.* p. 245.
34. Bowlby, *Making and Breaking*, pp. 136–141.
35. Mary Ainsworth, "The Development of Infant-Mother Attachment," in *Review of Child Development Research*, ed. Bettye M. Caldwell and Henry N. Ricciuti (Chicago: University of Chicago Press, 1976), pp. 1–94.
36. Carnegie, *Starting Points*, p. 45.
37. Michael Rutter, *Maternal Deprivation Reassessed*, (New York: Penguin Books, 1981), p. 105.
38. T. Berry Brazelton, *Working and Caring*, (Redding, Massachusetts: Addison–Wesley Publishing Co., 1987), pp. 55–56.
39. Tiffany Field, quoted in an article by R. Trotter, "The Play's the Thing," *Psychology Today* (January 1987): p. 27.
40. Selma Fraiberg, *Every Child's Birthright: In Defense of Mothering*, (New York: Basic Books, 1977): p. 47.
41. P. Shaver, C. Hazen, and W. Bradshaw, "Love as an Attachment," *Psychology of Love*, ed. R. Sternberg and M. Barnes (New Haven, Connecticut: Yale University Press, 1989), p. 83.
42. Burton White, "Should You Stay Home with Your Baby?" *American Baby*, (October 1985): p. 27.
43. Magid and McKelvey, *High Risk*, p. 134.
44. John Bowlby, *Attachment and Loss*, vol. 2, *Separation Anxiety and Anger* (New York: Basic Books, 1973), p. 33.
45. E. Cummings and D. Cichetti, *Attachment in the Preschool Years*, ed. Greenberg (Chicago: University of Chicago Press, 1990), p. 345.
46. *Ibid.* p. 347.
47. *Ibid.* p. 353.
48. T. W. Moore, (1964) Children of Full-Time and Part-Time Mothers—*Int. J. Soc. Psychiatry*; Special Congress Issue no. 2: "Effects on the Children." In S. Yudkin & A. Holme (eds). *Working Mothers and Their Children*. Second edition. London: Sphere Books (1969)—Also reported in Bowlby: Separation (New York: Basic Books, 1973), p. 224.

49. Virginia Hunter, "John Bowlby: An Interview," *Psycho-analytic Review*, (Summer 1991) p. 166.
50. Weil, *Early Deprivation*, p. 142.
51. *Ibid.* p. 141.
52. Magid and McKelvey, *High Risk*, p. 119.

CHAPTER 6: WHY PARENTAL CARE IS WORTH IT

1. Carnegie, *Starting Points*, p. 9.
2. *Ibid.*
3. Naomi Baron, *Growing up with Language: How Children Learn To Talk* (Redding, Massachusetts: Addison–Wesley Publishing Co., 1992), p. 25.
4. *Ibid.* p. 86.
5. Francis Palgrave, *Love's Language*, (ca. 1861).
6. Dr. Sally Ward, Interview with Alexander Hobbs, *London Observer*, July 17, 1993. "TV and Hi-fi Noise Blamed for Child Speech Problems."
7. Dr. Sally Ward, Interview with Alexander Hobbs, *Manchester Guardian*, September 21, 1994: "Turn Off, Talk Up–Early Learning–Constant Television May Harm Your Child."
8. George Gerbner, "Is the Road Runner to Blame? Children, Violence and Television," Lecture at Univ. of Pennsylvania, Philadelphia, May 20, 1995.
9. Bruno Bettleheim, Lecture to Parents, Los Angeles, Calif., 1975.
10. Magid and McKelvey, *High Risk*, p. 246.
11. Fraiberg, *Every Child's Birthright*, p. 62.
12. Leach, *Children First*, p. 23.
13. *Ibid.* p. 27.
14. Karen Schachere, "Attachment Between Working Mothers and Their Infants: The Influence of Family Process," *American Journal of Orthopsychiatry* 60 (January, 1990): pp. 19–34.

CHAPTER 7: SOLUTIONS: HOW TO PROVIDE CONTINUITY OF QUALITY CARE

1. John Bowlby, *Maternal Care and Mental Health* (Geneva: World Health Organization 1951; New York: Schocken 1966) p. 49.
2. *Zero to Three* October/November, 1994 Vol. 15 No. 2 p. 13—Article by Hedy Nai-Lin Chang with Dora Pulido: *The Critical Importance of Cultural and Linguistic Continuity for Infants and Toddlers* (From California Tomorrow, San Francisco, California), quoting J. Ronald Lally, Director, Center for Child and Family Studies, Far West Laboratory; also adapted from *Affirming Childrens' Roots: Cultural and Linguistic Diversity in Early Care and Education.*
3. *Time Magazine* November 25, 1994.
4. Brazelton, *Working and Caring*, p. 116.
5. Carnegie, *Starting Points*, p. 45.
6. Whitebook, *Who Cares? Child Care Teachers and the Quality of Care in America*, p. 12.
7. Univ. of Colorado, Denver, *Cost*, pp. 71–72.
8. *Ibid.* pp. 25–26.
9. *Ibid.*
10. *Ibid.* p. 26.
11. *Ibid.* pp. 71–72.
12. Spock, *A Better World*, p. 14.
13. Carnegie, *Starting Points*, p. 45.
14. Mickey Butts, "Day Care Laws," *Parenting* (November 1993): p. 132.
15. Spock, *A Better World*, p. 143.
16. Whitebook, Howes, and Phillips, *Who Cares?* p. 12.
17. C. L. Coe, et al. "Endocrine and Immune Responses to Separation and Maternal Loss in Nonhuman Primates," in *The Psychobiology of Attachment and Separation*, eds. M. L. Reite, and T. Field, (New York: Academic Press, 1985), pp. 163–200. Cited in Dr. J. Craig Peery, "Children at Risk: The Case Against Day Care," *The Family in America* (February, 1991).

18. David M. Bell, "Illness Associated With Child Day Care," A Study of Incidence and Cost. *American Journal of Public Health* 79 (1989): pp. 479–484. Cited in Dr. J. Craig Peery, "Children at Risk: The Case Against Day Care," *The Family in America* (February, 1991).

19. L. J. Anderson, "Daycare Center Attendance and Hospitalization for Lower Respiratory Tract Illness," *Pediatrics* 82 (1988): pp. 300–307. Cited in Dr. J. Craig Peery, "Children at Risk: The Case Against Day Care," *The Family in America* (February, 1991).

20. R. E. Black, et al., "Giardiasis in Day Care Centers: Evidence of Person-to-Person Transmission," *Pediatrics* 60 (1977): pp. 486–491; A. B. Doyle, "Incidence of Illness in Early Group and Family Day Care," *Pediatrics* 58 (1976): pp. 607–613; P. S. Sullivan, et al., "Longitudinal Study of Occurrence of Diarrheal Disease in Day Care Centers," *American Journal of Public Health* 74 (1984): pp. 987–999; Stelcette, "Recurrent Outbreaks of Giardiasis in a Child Day Care Center," pp. 485–490. Cited in Dr. J. Craig Peery, "Children at Risk: The Case Against Day Care," *The Family in America* (February, 1991).

21. Child Day Care Infectious Disease Study Group, "Public Health Considerations of Infectious Diseases in Child Day Care Centers," *Journal of Pediatrics* 105 (1984): pp. 683–701. Cited in Dr. J. Craig Peery, "Children at Risk: The Case Against Day Care," *The Family in America* (February, 1991).

22. Bell, "Illness Associated with Child Day Care," pp. 479–484.

23. Spock, *A Better World,* p. 14.

CHAPTER 8: FINAL THOUGHTS ON "BEING THERE"

1. Hunter, "An Interview," p. 167.

Bibliography

Ainsworth, Mary D., et al. *Patterns of Attachment: A Psychological Study of the Strange Situation.* Hillsdale, N.J.: Erlbaum, 1978.

———. "The Development of Infant-Mother Attachment." In *Review of Child Development and Research*, Vol. 3, edited by B. M. Caldwell and H. N. Ricciuti, 1–94. Chicago: University of Chicago Press, 1973.

———. *Infancy in Uganda: Infant Care and the Growth of Love.* Baltimore: Johns Hopkins Univ. Press, 1967.

Anderson, L. J. "Daycare Center Attendance and Hospitalization for Lower Respiratory Tract Illness." *Pediatrics* 82 (1988): 300–307.

Barglow, Peter. "Some Further Comments About Infant Day-Care Research." *Zero to Three* (June 1987).

Baron, Naomi. *Growing up with Language: How Children Learn to Talk.* Redding, Mass.: Addison–Wesley: 1992.

Barton and Schwartz. "Daycare in the Middle Class—Effects and Elementary School." Paper presented to APA Annual Convention, Los Angeles, 1981.

Bell, David M. "Illness Associated with Child Daycare, A Study of Incidence and Cost." *American Journal of Public Health* 79 (1989): 479–484.

Belsky, J. "The 'Effects' of Infant Daycare Reconsidered." *Early Childhood Research Quarterly* 3 (1988): 235–272.

———. "Infant Daycare: A Cause for Concern." *Zero to Three* (September 1986).

"Risks Remain." *Zero to Three* (February 1987).

Belsky, J., and Michael Rovin. "Nonmaternal Care in the First Year of Life and the Security of Infant-Parent Attachment." *Child Development* 59 (1988): 157–167.

Belsky, J., A. Voneye, and R. A. Isabella. "Origins of Infant-Mother Attachment: An Examination of International Synchrony During the Infant's First Year." *Developmental Psychology* 25 (1989): New York: 112–121.

Black, R. E., et al. "Giardiasas in Day Care Centers: Evidence of Person-to-Person Transmission." *Pediatrics* 60 (1977): 486–491.

Bowlby, John, *Attachment and Loss,* vol. 1, *Attachment.* New York: Basic Books, 1969.

———. "Attachment and Loss: Retrospect and Prospect." *American Journal of Orthopsychiatry* 52 no. 4 (October 1982).

———. *A Secure Base.* New York: Basic Books, 1988.

———. "Forty-Four Juvenile Thieves." *International Journal of Psychoanalysis* 25: 19–52; 107–127. Reprinted 1946 (Monograph) Gordon Bailiere, Tindall & Cox.

———. *Attachment and Loss,* vol. 3, *Loss.* New York: Basic Books, 1980.

———. *The Making and Breaking of Affectional Bonds.* London: Tavistock Publications, 1979.

———. "Maternal Care and Mental Health." *Monograph Series* no. 2 (Geneva: World Health Organization, 1951).

———. *Attachment and Loss,* vol. 2, *Separation.* Basic Books, New York: 1973.

Brazelton, T. B. *Working and Caring.* Redding, Mass.: Addison–Wesley, 1987.

Bretherton, Inge. *The Roots and Growing Points of Attachment Theory (The Nature of Attachment).* 1991.

Butts, Mickey. "Day Care Laws." *Parenting,* November, 1993, 132.

Carnegie Corporation. *Starting Points: Meeting the Needs of Our Youngest Children.* New York: Carnegie Corporation, 1994.

Chang, Hedy Nai-Lin. "The Critical Importance of Cultural and Linguistic Continuity for Infants and Toddlers." *Zero to Three* 15, no. 2 (National Center for Clinical Infant Programs, Arlington, Va., 1994): 13.

Children's Defense Fund. *The State of America's Children Yearbook.* Washington, D.C.: Children's Defense Fund, 1995.

"Children At Risk: The Case Against Day Care" *The Family of America* Issue Feb 19, 1991 vol. 5, #2.

Cline, F. *Understanding and Treating the Severely Disturbed Child*; Evergreen, Colorado, 1979.

Cole, Cynthia, and Hyman Rodman. "When School Age Children Care for Themselves: Issues for Family Life Educators and Parents." *Family Relations* 36 (January 1987): 92–96.

Cummings, E. M. and D. Cichetti. *Attachment in the Preschool Years*. Chicago: University of Chicago Press, 1990.

Diehl, I. "The Prevalence of Colds in Nursery School Children and Non Nursery School Children." *Journal of Pediatrics* 34 (1949): 52–61.

Dobson, J. and G. L. Bauer. *Children at Risk*. Dallas: Word Publishing Co., 1990.

Doyle, A. B. "Incidence of Illness in Early Group and Family Day Care. *Pediatrics* 58 (1976): 607–613.

Eggebeen, D. J. and A. J. Hawkins. "Economic Need and Wives' Employment." *Journal of Family Issues* (1990): 38–66.

Elkind, A. *The Hurried Child*. Redding, Mass.: Addison–Welsey, 1981.

Erickson, M. F., L. A. Sroufe, and V. Egland. *The Relationship Between Quality of Attachment and Behavior Problems in Preschool in a High Risk Sample*. Monographs of the Society for Research and Child Development, 1985, Vol. 50 (p. 147–166).

Fahlberg, V. *Attachment and Separation: Putting the Pieces Together*. Michigan Department of Social Services Publication 429, (Ann Arbor, Michigan: Michigan Department of Social Services, 1979).

Flemming, and others. "Childhood Upper Respiratory Tract Infections: To What Degree Is Incidence Affected by Day Care Attendance." *Pediatrics* 79 (1987): 55–60.

Fortune Magazine, May 20, 1991, "Can Your Career Hurt Your Kids?"

Fraiberg, S. *Every Child's Birthright: In Defense of Mothering*. New York: Basic Books, 1977.

———. *The Magic Years*. New York: Charles Scribner's Sons, 1959.

Hamilton, Victoria. "Some Problems in the Clinical Application of Attachment Theory." *Psychoanalytic Psychotherapy* 3, no. 1 (1987).

Haskins, R. "Public School Aggression Amongst Children With Varying Daycare Experience (University of North Carolina—Frances Parker Study). *Child Development* 56: 689–703.

Heath, Harriet. "A Good Reference for Parents." *Zero To Three* 1987: 25 (Special Reprint of Feb. 1987 article).

Henry, Sherry. "They Fight to Protect Their Children." *Parade Magazine* (March 18, 1990): 5.

Howes, Carollee. "University of California Study." *Newsweek Special Issue,* Winter/Spring 1990, 92.

Hunter, Virginia. "John Bowlby: An Interview." *Psychoanalytic Review* 78, no. 2 (Summer 1991).

Jacobson, Arminta, and Susan Owen. "Infant Caregiver Interactions in Day Care." *Child Study Journal* (1987): 197–209.

Jacobvitz, D. and L. A. Sroufe. "The Early Caregiver-Child Relationship and Attention-Deficit Disorder with Hyperactivity in Kindergarten." *Child Development* 58 (1987): 1496–1504.

Karen, R. "Becoming Attached: What Children Need." *The Atlantic*: February 2, (1990): 35–70.

Kestenbaum, R., E. Farber, and L. A. Sroufe. "Individual Differences in Empathy Among Preschoolers: Relation to Attachment History." *New Direction for Child Development* 44, San Francisco Jossey-Bass, Summary (1989): 52–56.

Kobak, R., and J. Cassidy. "Avoidance and Its Relation to Other Defensive Processes." Edited by J. Belsky and T. Nezworski: in *Clinical Implications of Attachment.* Hillsdale: Lawrence Erlbaum, 1988.

Konner, M. "The Enigmatic Smile." *Psychology Today* (March, 1987): 42–44.

Lamb, M. "Parent-Infant Interaction, Attachment and Socioemotional Development in Infancy." In *The Development of Attachment and Affiliative Systems,* edited by R. Emde and R. Harmon. New York: Plenum Press, 1982.

Leach, Penelope. *Children First: What Our Society Must Do and Is Not Doing for Our Children*. New York: Knopf, 1994.

Magid, K., and C. McKelvey. *High Risk: Children Without a Conscience*. New York: Bantam Books, 1988.

Mooney, Clark, Martin, and Lloyd. "Type of Childcare at 18 Months: Differences in Interactional Experience." *Journal of Child Psychiatry and Allied Disciplines*. (1990): 849.

Moore, T. W. "Children of Full-Time and Part-Time Mothers." *International Journal of Social Psychiatry* (Special Congressional Issue No. 2, 1964).

National Center for Clinical Infant Programs, Arlington, Virginia. *Zero to Three*—Special Reprint (Articles Sept. 1986 and Feb. 1987).

Newsweek. "How Kids Grow" (Summer, 1991).

Norris, and Miller. *The Working Mother's Complete Handbook*. New York: Sunrise/E. P. Dutton, 1979.

Parkes, and Stevenson-Hinde. *The Place of Attachment in Human Behavior*. New York: Basic Books, 1982.

Peery, J. Craig. "Children at Risk: The Case Against Day Care." *The Family in America* 5, no. 2 (February 1991).

Phillips, D., McCartney, K., Scarr, S., and Howes, C. "Selective Review of Infant Daycare Research: A Cause for Concern." *Zero To Three* (February and June, 1987).

Powell, Douglas R. "After-School Childcare." *Young Children* (March 1987): 62–66.

Robertson, J. *A Two Year Old Goes to the Hospital*. University Park: Pennsylvania State University Audio Visual Services, 1953.

Rutter, M. *Maternal Deprivation Reassessed*. New York: Penguin Books, 1981.

———. "Socio-Emotional Consequences of Day Care for Preschool Children." *American Journal of Orthopsychiatry* (1981): 9–11.

Shapiro, and Hadler. "Risks of Anteric Infection Associated with Child Daycare (Hepatitis A and Hepatitis B Virus Infections in Daycare Settings)." *Pediatric Annals* 20 (1991): 403–441.

Shaver, Philip, C. Hazan, and W. D. Bradshaw. "Love As Attachment." In *Psychology of Love*, edited by Sternberg, R. and Barnes, M.: New Haven, Connecticut: Yale University Press, 1988.

Spitz, R. A. "Hospitalism: An Inquiry Into the Genesis of Psychiatric Conditions in Early Childhood." *Psychoanalytic Study of the Child* 1 (1945): 53–74.

Spock, Benjamin. *A Better World for Our Children*. Bethesda: National Press Books, 1994.

Sroufe, L. A. "Appraisal: Bowlby's Contribution to Psychoanalytic Theory and Developmental Psychology; Attachment: Separation: Loss." *Journal of Child Psychology and Psychiatry*. 27, no. 6 1986: 841–849.

Sroufe, Cooper, DeHart, and Marshal. *Child Development*. 2d ed. New York: McGraw Hill, Inc., 1992.

Sroufe, L. A. and E. Waters. "Heart Rate as a Convergent Measure in Clinical and Developmental Reserach." *Merrill-Palmer Quarterly* 23 (1977): 3–27.

Stelcette, R. W. "Recurrent Outbreaks of Giardiasis in a Child Day Care Center, Wisconsin." *American Journal of Public Health* 79 (1989): 485–490.

Stern, Daniel. *Diary of a Baby*. New York: Basic Books, 1990.

———. *Interpersonal World of the Infant*. New York: Basic Books, 1985.

Sullivan, P. S., et al. "Longitudinal Study of Occurrence of Diarrheal Disease in Day Care Centers." *American Journal of Public Health* 74 (1974): 987–999.

Suomi, S. J., and H. F. Harlow. 1971. Abnormal Social Behavior in Young Monkeys. In *Exceptional Infant*. Vol. 2, ed. J. Helmuth. New York: Bruner/Mazel.

Thompson, Ross A. *Attachment Theory and Daycare Research*. Washington, D.C.: National Center Clinical Infant Programs, December, 1987.

Trotter, R. J. "The Play's the Thing." *Psychology Today* (January 1987): 27.

University of Colorado, Denver. *Cost, Quality and Child Outcomes Study Team: Cost, Quality and Child Outcomes in*

Child Care Centers. 2d ed. Denver: Univ. of Colorado Economics Department, 1995.

Vandel, D., and A. Corasaniti. "Variations in Early Childcare: Do They Predict Subsequent Social, Emotional and Cognitive Differences?" *New Directions in Child Development* (1990).

Ward, Sally. "Interview and Articles" by Andrew Hobbs in *London Observer* July 17, 1993 and *Manchester Guardian* September 21, 1994.

Weil, John L. *Early Deprivation of Empathic Care.* Madison: International Universities Press, 1992.

Werner, Emmy. "High Risk Children in Young Adulthood: A Longitudinal Study from Birth to 32 Years." *American Journal of Orthropsychiatry* 59 (January 1989): 75–76.

White, Burton. *Hard Truths About Day Care* by Karl Zinsmeister (quotation); *Readers Digest,* (October 1988): 90.

———. "Should You Stay Home With Your Baby?" *American Baby* (October, 1985): 27.

Whitebook, M., C. Howes, and D. Phillips. "Who Cares? Childcare Teachers and the Quality of Care in America." *The National Childcare Staffing Study.* Oakland, Calif.: Childcare Employee Project, 1989.

Winnicott, D. W. *The Maturational Processes and the Facilitating Environment.* New York: International University Press, 1965.

Zigler, Edward. *Recommendations of the Advisory Committee of Infant Care Leave.* New Haven, Connecticut: Yale Bush Center, 1985.

Index